# The Complete Guide to Siberian Huskies

Mary Meisenzahl

Publication Data

Mary Meisenzahl

The Complete Guide to Siberian Huskies ---- First edition.

Summary: "Successfully raising a Siberian Husky dog from puppy to old age" --- Provided by publisher.

ISBN: 978-1-09640-701-0

[1. Siberian Huskies --- Non-Fiction] I. Title.

This book has been written with the published intent to provide accurate and authoritative information in regard to the subject matter included. While every reasonable precaution has been taken in preparation of this book the author and publisher expressly disclaim responsibility for any errors, omissions, or adverse effects arising from the use or application of the information contained inside. The techniques and suggestions are to be used at the reader's discretion and are not to be considered a substitute for professional veterinary care. If you suspect a medical problem with your dog, consult your veterinarian.

Design by Sorin Rădulescu

First paperback edition, 2019

# TABLE OF CONTENTS

# CHAPTER 1
# Siberian Husky

Siberian Huskies are one of the most recognizable dog breeds, known for their striking wolf-like features. They've become popular on the internet as videos of them howling, playing, and pulling sleds have gone viral. But what exactly makes a Husky a Husky?

## What is a Husky?

Huskies are medium-sized dogs, classified as a working breed. They are members of the Spitz family, along with other breeds thought to originate from the Arctic region and Siberia including Shiba Inus, Pomeranians, and Klee Klais. Spitzes are distinguishable for their thick coats, white fur, and curled or drooping tails.

As a working breed, which is a catchall category for dogs whose purpose does not fit into another category such as herding, Huskies were bred for pulling sleds.

They aren't ideal for first-time owners, but they can make a great pet for an experienced dog lover.

*Photo Courtesy of Sheila Smith*

# History of the Husky

Siberian Huskies date back thousands of year to the Chukchi people in Siberia. They used the sled dogs to assist in hunting reindeer and for pulling loads for long distances to survive in the harsh, cold climate in pursuit of food. Once the Chukchi successfully domesticated some reindeer, sled dogs were also bred to herd them. The reindeer were then used to pull the heaviest loads, and sled dogs were bred for endurance and agility, rather than purely for strength. Huskies today are descended from these original sled dogs. This has made them extraordinarily fast at pulling light loads long distances, even with little food.

**HELPFUL TIP**
**From Siberia to Alaska**

The Siberian Husky was brought from Siberia to Alaska in 1908 during the Nome gold rush to work as a sled dog transporting people and materials through Alaska. Soon, sled dog teams full of Huskies started winning sled dog competitions like the Annual All-Alaska Sweepstakes, cementing this breed's popularity.

The term "Husky" is thought to come from the name "Esky," which was once applied to Eskimos and then extended to their dogs.

In 1908, dogs from Russia were imported to Alaska to be used as sled dogs during the gold rush and in the "All-Alaska Sweepstakes," a 408-mile sled dog ride. Siberian Huskies excelled in this type of competition over the heavier freighting dogs typically used in Alaska, due to their speed and endurance.

Huskies are perhaps best remembered in popular culture for another run in Alaska: carrying diphtheria medicine to Nome, as depicted in the 1995 film Balto.

In January 1925, two children had already died of a diphtheria epidemic in Nome, and the city's supply of serum was exhausted. The nearest serum was 1000 miles away in Anchorage. Trains could get the serum about 600 miles from Nome, and no further. Few had the skills and experience to fly in the winter, and severe winds and blizzards made travel nearly impossible.

Sled dogs were the only option to get the medications to Nome in time. Leonard Seppala, winner of the All-Alaska Sweepstakes, ran his Siberian Husky team for 261 miles over the most dangerous part of the trail, led by his Husky Togo. The final leg of the relay was led by Balto, another Siberian Husky, who guided the team back on track after becom-

Photo Courtesy of
Elena Martinez

ing lost on ice. Balto led the team through portions of the trail with such poor visibility that the musher couldn't even see the dogs in front of him.

Balto and Togo were honored as heroes, and a statue of Balto was erected in Central Park. The inscription reads: "Dedicated to the indomitable spirit of the sled dogs that relayed antitoxin six hundred miles over rough ice, across treacherous waters, through Arctic blizzards from Nenana to the relief of stricken Nome in the winter of 1925. Endurance. Fidelity. Intelligence." Balto received more praise and recognition, although many mushers consider Togo the real hero of the race, running almost twice as far as any other team. The Iditarod, a sled dog race from Anchorage to Nome that began in 1973, was inspired by this run.

Balto and Togo's teams both toured the United States and drew large crowds. Seppala sold most of his team to a kennel in Maine, and most U.S. Huskies today are descended from one of these dogs.

In 1930, the Siberian Husky was recognized by the American Kennel Club (AKC). Navy Rear Admiral Richard E. Byrd took 50 Huskies on a 16,000-mile trek around the coast of Antarctica in 1933, proving again their ability to work in extreme environments. The U.S. Army also used Huskies in its Arctic Search and Rescue Unit during World War II.

Since then, and into the 21st century, Siberian Huskies have proven to be popular pets. In 2017, the AKC ranked them the 12th most popular breed.

# Physical Characteristics

Siberian Huskies are medium-sized dogs with compact bodies. They tend to be muscular, and hold their heads up high with straight backs. Males are usually between 45 and 60 pounds, and females usually are 35 to 50 pounds.

Siberian Huskies have a distinct look that contributes to their popularity as pets. They have a thick double coat, triangular ears, and distinctive color markings. Bred to survive in the Arctic and endure severe temperatures, their double coat consists of a dense undercoat and a coarse, straight top coat. These coats both protect Huskies from cold temperatures and reflect heat. Husky coats are usually white at the paws, legs, face, and tail tips. The rest of their coat is typically black and white, and less commonly, gray and white, red and white, or pure white. Facial markings can vary considerably.

Photo Courtesy of
Joelle Brown

*Photo Courtesy of*
*John Sieber*

Heavy coats lead to fur shedding year-round, with two major sheds each year, and require at least weekly grooming. As a plus, though, Huskies are very clean dogs who rarely smell, and will often spend hours grooming themselves and cleaning their feet.

The AKC describes the eyes of Siberian Huskies as "an almond shape, moderately spaced, and set slightly oblique." Their eyes are blue, brown, or black. Many Huskies are distinctive for their heterochromatic eyes, meaning the eyes are two different colors. Parti-colored eyes involve a mostly blue eye that has a speck of brown, or vice versa. Be careful about choosing a puppy based on eye color though—many puppies start out with blue eyes, and one or both turn brown by the time they are eight weeks old.

Huskies have long muzzles with noses that can appear black on gray dogs, tan on black dogs, liver on red dogs, and light tan on white dogs. Some Siberian Huskies also exhibit hypopigmentation, or snow nose. This is a condition in which parts of the nose lighten during cold weather. For some dogs, this only happens in the winter and their nose returns to its regular color the rest of the year, while other dogs retain their light pink color.

Siberian Husky tails are usually bushy with a white tip, and can be quite expressive. When the Husky is relaxed, the tail will hang low, and when she is excited or interested in something, the tail will curve up in a sickle shape. Tails can be so curly that they reach a dog's back.

When Huskies sleep, they will often curl up and cover their noses and faces with their tails. This position, which conserves warmth, is known as a "Siberian Swirl."

# Breed Behavioral Characteristics

*"Huskies are extremely non-aggressive and do not make good watch dogs at all. They love everyone. We jokingly tell people that all of our dogs have their 'licker license'."*

**Bonnie Schaeffel**
*Liberty Siberians*

While many of their behaviors are typical to other breeds, Siberian Huskies do have some distinct behaviors and traits that are crucial to know before you decide to bring one into your home. I'll explain these in more detail later, but here's a quick look into the basic behaviors of the breed.

Siberian Huskies are somewhat famous on the internet for one aspect of their behavior: howling. Huskies often howl instead of barking as

*Photo Courtesy of
Anthony Couture*

a means of communication, and they'll howl to let you know they want attention or something else from you. It can also be a sign of separation anxiety, or a response to a noise outside like a siren.

Breeder Jess Moore of Jalerran Siberians says, "They are not trustworthy off-lead; they're escape artists." As dogs bred to work, Huskies are extremely strong and intelligent. When their physical and mental energy is not used up, they take it out on your home/shoes/yard. Clever and energetic can be a dangerous mix, especially when combined with their instincts to roam, so Huskies are known to get into trouble, steal food, and find ways to escape just about any enclosure. Because of these traits, at least a six-foot fence is recommended for outdoor enclosures, although Huskies have been known to make it over fences as tall as eight feet. Electric pet fences are not recommended for the breed. Depending on an individual dog's temperament, it may not do well if left alone inside for long periods of time, where Huskies are prone to destroy things. Huskies maintain their puppy playfulness well into adulthood, and they need stimulation and outlets for their playful energy.

Bred as pack animals, Siberian Huskies crave and love companionship. They like to be part of your family, and should get along well with

other dogs. In general, Huskies won't be content to be left alone for long periods of time or enjoy being confined to a separate part of the house. They may be clingy and stick close by, following you around the house. However, they are also independent and stubborn and like to cuddle and spend time together on their own terms. Though they aren't lapdogs and can't be forced into snuggling, they'll be happiest with the option to stay close to the family. Because of their independence, Huskies can be particularly difficult to train. They are stubborn, and often don't like to take orders without a treat.

Siberian Huskies are natural predators, with a strong prey drive. They usually can't be trusted outside without a leash because they will be tempted to chase after birds, small animals, or anything else that catches their eye.

Despite this natural drive for prey, Siberian Huskies are

## FUN FACT
**Balto**

In 1925, Leonhard Seppala raced a relay team of Huskies 658 miles to Nome, Alaska, in only five and a half days to rush life-saving diphtheria treatments to the town. The lead dog on the final leg of the journey, Balto, is regarded as a hero. There is a statue of him in New York City, and an animated movie with two sequels was made about his legacy.

not aggressive. According to breeder Bonnie Schaeffel of Liberty Siberians, "They are extremely nonaggressive and do not make good watchdogs at all. They love everyone." They don't make good guard dogs because they are naturally friendly and greet strangers. They tend not to be territorial, and don't usually bark at people or animals.

With their nonaggressive and affectionate natures, Huskies are classified by the ASPCA as good with children. They enjoy being part of your family pack and will welcome children into the pack.

# Is a Husky the Right Fit for You?

*"Siberian Huskies are not good apartment dwellers. They need daily exercise and consistency in their training. A bored Husky is bound to find trouble."*

**Jill n Kenn Campbell**
*Campbell's Siberian Huskies*

This may seem like an overload of information, but all of these points are important considerations before you invite a Husky into your home. Adopting and training a Husky are major commitments, and they live 12 to 14 years on average. Before you make the decision, ask yourself if you're willing to put up with the more difficult and negative traits for at least that length of time.

- Do you have experience as a dog owner?
- Do you live in a place with a cool climate, or if you don't, are you able to provide shade and air conditioning?
- Can you provide the space and exercise an active Husky will require?
- Can you be firm and consistent in training your Husky?
- Are you willing to commit to thorough weekly grooming?
- Will your Husky be able to spend much or most of its time with you and your family?

If you can confidently answer "yes" to all of these questions, then you might be in a good place to adopt a Husky. Putting up with extreme shedding, destructive tendencies, and potential escapes can give you over a decade of love from a dog that will show loyalty and fun.

Before you adopt a Husky, it's important to take an honest look at your lifestyle and how accommodating it will be to a Husky's needs. For example, if you already lead an active life and enjoy hiking or walking, a Siberian Husky will easily fit into this routine and will benefit from the exercise. A more sedentary lifestyle, on the other hand, might lead to a bored and restless dog that misbehaves.

Someone who works from home, or is home often to spend time with a Husky is a good candidate for adoption, because they don't do well if left by themselves for too long. Potential owners who travel often may not be a good fit, and could lead to separation anxiety in the Husky.

You should also consider where you live. Although they are not huge dogs, Huskies do require space and will do better in the suburbs or rural areas than in the city. A house will give them more space than an apartment, and having a yard is beneficial.

While you should think about the area and home you could provide to a Husky, also be sure to consider the climate. If the area where you live is warm at any time of the year, you should be able to provide a cool area for activities and rest for your Husky. You will likely require a bigger indoor area for your Husky if your climate is warm, because they do not tolerate extended periods in hot weather very well.

You should only move forward in adopting a Husky after you have seriously considered all of these Husky needs, as well as anything else that might be specific to your situation. When you're confident you can provide all of this, and you have the spare money for food, toys, vet bills, and whatever else may come up, you're probably ready to adopt a Husky! If you're committed to loving and taking care of your Husky, you'll almost certainly be rewarded by a loyal and affectionate friend who, while not necessarily the cuddliest dog in the world, will show you her love and appreciation at being a part of your family.

# CHAPTER 2
# **Choosing a Husky**

Okay, so you've read up on the breed and decided to get one. You've made your peace with shedding, destruction, and an independent dog. Now, how do you pick the right one? In this chapter, we'll go over what to look for and how to find the right dog for your family. Ultimately, though, there is no one single match made in heaven. If you follow these steps, treat your dog with care, and train him carefully, you can have a wonderful relationship.

*Photo Courtesy of*
*Sandy Murphy*

# Buying vs. Adopting

With a breed as popular as Siberian Huskies, you will probably be able to find dogs from breeders and shelters in your area. But which is right for you?

Huskies are often surrendered to shelters when owners find that the howling, shedding, or exercise needs are more of a burden than they anticipated. As a result, many slightly older Huskies are sometimes available from shelters.

Purebred Siberian Huskies can be expensive, so one reason to consider adopting from a shelter is the cost. Usually, your adoption fee covers vaccinations, spaying or neutering, microchipping, deworming, and other necessary health procedures, so you save having to pay for all of these individual procedures yourself.

If you choose to adopt from a shelter, you know that you aren't accidentally supporting a puppy mill or other unethical organization. Your local shelter's dogs might vary, but you should also look for a Siberian Husky-specific rescue.

Adopting a Husky from a shelter can be good from a financial and moral standpoint, but there are reasons to consider a breeder, too. A good breeder will provide a loving and healthy environment for their dogs. A major benefit of buying from a breeder is the extra information available to you. What are the dog's parents like? Is there a history of health problems? What kind of temperaments run in the family? When adopting from a shelter, you probably won't have much background information on how your dog was raised or what her parents were like.

Ultimately, the choice is yours. Great pets come from both breeders and shelters. If you do decide to buy from a breeder, be sure to keep reading for help choosing the right one.

Photo Courtesy of Chelsee Taylor

# How to Find a Reputable Breeder

*"Do your research about the breed. Siberian huskies are not for everyone. Use the Siberian Husky Club of America (https://www.shca.org/ ) breeder referral list to choose a breeder. Be sure to choose a breeder who tests the dogs and certifies them free of hereditary hip and eye diseases. You can verify that they do that testing using OFA.org website."*

**Sheri Wright**
*Bralin Siberian Huskies*

There are many ways to start your search for the right breeder. Because you're probably an experienced dog owner if you're in the market for a Husky, ask your vet for a referral. You could also get a referral from local Siberian Husky clubs, or by visiting professional dog shows.

# Choosing a Breeder

A quick Google search will reveal many breeders, and choosing the right one can be intimidating. You want to find someone who is knowledgeable, caring, and up to AKC standards. Breeder Liane Tofani of Midnight White Siberians says, "All Siberians are beautiful, but they are not all raised the same. Choosing the breeder should be just as important as the puppy. Research is KEY." Here's what you should look for:

You should definitely be allowed to visit the premises and see what the breeder's setup looks like. If they don't allow you to do this, consider it a major red flag. Is the kennel clean? Are there bad odors? Are the animals active, lively, and friendly? Are there any signs of illness or protruding ribs? Take note of all of these conditions, and trust your gut. If something feels off, this might not be the best choice.

When you visit, you should ask, or the breeder should offer to meet the puppies' parents. Besides seeing the living conditions of the older dogs, you'll also have a look at the likely future health and appearance of your puppy.

Pay attention to the way that the dogs, both puppies and adults, interact with the breeder. The breeder should appear to genuinely care for the puppies and take an interest in their well-being. Dogs should be playful and excited around breeder, not timid.

*Photo Courtesy of Brianna Uherec & Kyle Sylvia*

A constant supply of puppies is one red flag to be on the lookout for. If they always have puppies available, a breeder is probably not giving each dog the attention it needs and may be overbreeding dogs without giving them the rest and care they require. On the other hand, a reputable breeder may keep a waitlist of potential buyers for when they do have a litter.

A responsible breeder should be a great resource for you on Siberian Huskies and a mentor if you need help. If your breeder seems proactive about taking on this role, that's great. Breeders should be authorities on Husky-specific genetic diseases, and willing to discuss positive and negative aspects of the breed. Look for depth rather than breadth—a breeder who is raising several different breeds is probably not a Husky specialist. If they're a good breeder, they will likely encourage you to call them at any point in your dog's life if you need advice, and they may even have you sign a contract stating that if you become unable to care for the dog, she must be returned to them.

Your breeder should be able and eager to answer any questions you have, and provide additional insight and tips. They should also ask you questions and appear to want their dogs to go to safe, loving homes. Again, your gut feeling is important here. If a breeder is conversational and willing to talk with you about any concerns or thoughts that come up, that's a great sign. You should be comfortable talking to them. Remember, a responsible breeder won't sell their dogs to anyone who shows up with the money to purchase a puppy—they'll want to check out the person and vet them.

No knowledgeable breeder will let you bring the puppy home earlier than eight weeks old, and you shouldn't agree to take a younger puppy. Once your puppy is old enough, the breeder should give you proof of health screenings and AKC documentation of their pedigree, or "papers."

# Health Tests and Certifications

There are a few tests you should be sure to talk to your breeder about if they don't bring it up themselves. All Siberian Huskies used for breeding, not just show dogs, should have documentation of these tests. These tests ensure puppies have the highest likelihood of being free of genetic defects.

First, you should insist that your Husky's eyes are certified healthy. Either a Canine Eye Registration Form (CERF) or Siberian Husky Ophthalmological Registry (SHOR) are acceptable. For CERF, a canine ophthal-

Photo Courtesy of
Jenica Cunanan

mologist checks the dog's eyes for cataracts, corneal dystrophy, and other hereditary defects. These exams should be done annually because diseases can show up later in life and must be done within a year of breeding for the results to be considered valid. SHOR is a lower-cost option for eye testing. This option also certifies a dog's healthy eyes after she has been cleared of inherited eye diseases. These tests help to ensure that your puppy has a low risk of developing eye disorders as she grows.

You should also ask your breeder about an Orthopedic Foundation for Animals (OFA) hip certification. Siberian Huskies have a greater-than-average risk for hip dysplasia. This test is based on hip x-rays and thyroid tests, which should take place after age two. For this reason, Huskies should never be bred before they are two. OFA rates hips as excellent, good, or fair if they are non-dysplastic, or mildly, moderately, and severely dysplastic. Unlike eye tests, this only needs to be done once in a Husky's life.

Both of these tests are important for understanding the future health of your puppy. They are also good indicators about the type of breeder you're working with. A responsible breeder should bring these up without you asking, and should be happy to explain exactly what they mean to you.

# Breeder Contracts and Guarantees

When you buy your dog from a breeder, you will sign a contract that outlines some rights and requirements that may last the life of your dog. A reputable breeder should be willing to go through the terms with you and explain what each term means, and why it's important.

First of all, your contract will include a bill of sale. This states that you purchased the dog from your breeder. It may include state-specific clauses, including that the breeder is required to refund you within 24 hours if the pet becomes sick.

You should also receive an AKC registration application. Although breeders cannot register your pet with the AKC themselves, they should fill in the application for you, which includes their signature. You will also need information on your dog's breed, sex, color, date of birth, parents, and other facts.

Many breeders will include some kind of health clause in a contract. They may guarantee good health for a certain period of time, usually one or two years. In return, they will probably ask that you see a vet when your dog exhibits any symptoms or problems, and they might want to track health problems in their lineage. Some breeders even include a necropsy requirement if the dog dies without a diagnosis from a veterinarian.

Your contract will probably include a section on reproduction and breeding. Unless you bought your dog to compete in shows, the breeder will require that you spay or neuter your pet by a certain age. Or, they may allow you to breed your dog, unless they determine at some point in the future that the dog does not exhibit the breed standard. They

*Photo Courtesy of Ash Summers*

could also require that you not breed the dog until it is at least two years old, when most genetic problems will have revealed themselves.

More specific breeding rules could be part of contracts for show dogs. For example, your breeder may guarantee that your dog is fertile and free from inheritable diseases and defects. In return, they might require that you show the dog for a certain period of time before breeding her.

Many contracts include clauses regarding giving up your dog. You may be required to inform your breeder if you plan to rehome your dog, or if you can no longer care for her. Breeders like to keep track of their dogs throughout their lives to monitor for genetic health problems. They also are likely to have a wide network of people who could potentially take in your dog. In many cases, the breeder will agree to take in your dog if you no longer can.

# Choosing the Perfect Pup

Once you've done your research and decided a Siberian Husky is for you, you have to make the ultimate decision of choosing which pup to take home. There is no perfect puppy, and different temperaments will work better with different families, but here I'll provide some general guidelines to help you make a good pick.

First of all, are you looking for a male or a female? Speaking in generalizations, males tend to be more outgoing and affectionate, but also difficult to train. If you have another male dog, you might not want to bring home a male because they could fight for dominance. A female Husky may be more reserved than a male, but also easier to train. These do not hold true for every dog, but they are something to consider.

You'll want to examine the litter for temperament. You should observe the puppies as they play together. Some puppies might be eager to jump on you and climb all over, while others are timid and may shy away from you. Behaviors like these might be cute in short bursts, but try to think about how they will play out in your life long-term. Can you deal with a dog that is constantly high energy and jumping on everything? Or do you want a dog that's scared of everything? A puppy with a more moderate temperament is often more appealing.

You should also examine any puppies you are considering by themselves, away from their litters. A puppy that seems shy around his littermates may come out of his shell playing with you, for example. Before choosing a pup, definitely play with him one-on-one and hold him to see how he responds to you.

Most importantly, before buying any puppy you should perform your own quick examination for health. Make sure eyes are clear and without crust, and examine ears and nose for discharge. Puppies should also move without pain or soreness.

Finally, listen to the breeder. If you've chosen a breeder based on the criteria we outlined earlier, they've raised many puppies and generally know the temperaments of their dogs. They should be able to offer insight from longer observation than you've had, so they can tell you that the sleepy pup during your visit is actually the most rambunctious of the bunch, and not a good match for you. Once you've thought through all these aspects, it's time to pick your pup!

# Tips for Adopting a Husky

*"When rescuing an adult at a rescue, be sure to interact with the Husky. Huskies are VERY friendly by nature, and if one isn't friendly it may be a sign of past abuse. This doesn't mean they cannot be brought back to normal, it just means to make sure you know what you are getting into."*

**Andrew and Heather Kronenberger**
*Frosty Meadow Husky Farm*

Many of these tips are applicable for any breed, but some points are extra important for potential Husky owners.

Beware of puppy mills. Huskies are very popular for their wolf-like look, and not every breeder is ethical.

Insist on health certifications. At a minimum, your pup should come with assurances of healthy eyes and hips.

If you plan to adopt, find out everything you can about the dog's temperament from the shelter.

The more facetime you can put in with your puppy before adopting, the better! You'll get a feel for her personality and a better idea of what to expect. This also applies to the puppy's mother, whom you should try to spend time with if you can.

Keep in contact with your breeder, and stick with someone who is willing to have thorough conversations with you. They will be a great resource throughout your time as a Husky owner.

# CHAPTER 3
# Preparing Your Home for Your Siberian Husky

Y ou've picked out your pup! Now the fun (and the work) really begins. Save yourself some headaches and be as prepared as possible when you bring the newest member of your family home.

## Introducing Your Current Pets and Children

Photo Courtesy of Rebecca Hale

If you have other dogs, cats, or children, it's important to carefully plan their introduction to the new puppy.

Talking to your kids and preparing their expectations before the puppy comes home is crucial, especially if they are young or have never had a puppy before. Owning a middle-aged or elderly dog is very different from taking care of a puppy, and children should have a good idea of the differences going in.

Talk with your children about the right way to pet a puppy. If they're used to their older dog that is comfortable with them, this might be something to practice. Teach them how to get to know a new puppy—don't make sudden movements that might scare him, and offer him the back of your hand to sniff before doing anything else. If that goes okay, then remind them they can gently stroke the puppy's back and head. With kids and puppies both overexcited and jumping around, the puppy can easily get scared by a misplaced hand or an accidental touch to the eye. Don't be afraid to remind your kids how important being gentle and slow with the new puppy is.

Adjusting children's expectations to the way that puppies play is also hugely important to prevent disappointment. Your kids might be expecting a tiny puppy who immediately falls asleep in their lap, but puppies are usually full of energy and want to explore. In particular, puppies tend to try biting just about everything with their sharp baby teeth. Definitely warn your children that this will happen, and it doesn't mean your puppy is aggressive or doesn't like them! Just like a human baby, your puppy is still learning and exploring, and his mouth is the main way he can interact with the world.

Remind your kids that the biting phase will not last forever. Depending on their ages, you can also invite them to work with you to curb biting and teach the puppy. You and your kids are on the same team, so when you see something at biting level or catch your puppy in the act, your kids should know your plan to reprimand the puppy and reinforce the behavior.

Another surprise you'll have to impress on your kids will likely mean extra chores for them—potty training. Your kids should realize that the process takes time, and especially at first, someone will have to take the puppy out every hour, and also clean up any accidents inside. Depending on the age of your children, they might be excited at the chance to be helpers here. Be sure to discuss expectations for who will be taking the puppy out, or what the rotation schedule will be. Involve them in family conversations about how you will all have to be consistent about house-training.

Have your children practice saying "No" firmly, so that the puppy will learn to see them as an authority as well as their parents. Failure to do this can lead to the puppy obeying orders from adults, but not taking children seriously. Kids should also practice talking in quiet tones to prevent scaring the puppy.

Before bringing home your puppy, have several conversations about what bringing home a new puppy will mean for your family and your schedule. Everyone will have to be onboard in consistency about house-training, obedience, and not sneaking extra treats because the puppy is begging. Especially at first, the puppy will demand time and attention from everyone in the house. Make sure kids understand that sometimes the puppy will urgently need to go outside, for example. It's a good idea to have some space, like a bedroom or crate, that kids understand is off-limits for them and a place the pup can go to get away from all the action.

If you have other dogs, you'll want to prepare them as well. Before the introduction, put away your dog's favorite toys and treats to prevent territorial behavior. Make sure both dogs will have space in your home where they can be alone and away from each other. They should also have separate food and water dishes, and be fed separately.

# Dangerous Things that Dogs Might Eat or Encounter

*"Baby-proof your house! Siberians can be destructive when left unattended. If you don't want something chewed on, do not leave it lying around with a new Husky. It is important to know that it's never the puppies fault for chewing up your brand new Ugg Boots. It's your fault for not putting them out of reach."*

**Liane Tofani**
*Midnight White Siberians*

Puppy proofing your house is remarkably similar to babyproofing. Unfortunately, you don't have a few months where the baby is essentially unable to get into trouble or move without your help. From the second you bring your puppy home, basically everything in your house is a potential chew toy. Obviously, keeping your puppy in a totally empty room isn't practical or a particularly good idea, so let's focus on the most important items to keep out of your pup's reach.

Puppies use their noses and mouths to explore the world, so expect plenty of chewing and destruction. This is compounded by adopting

Huskies, who tend to be clever and enjoy getting into things that they're not supposed to. Later, we will get into what toys and supplies to have ready, but remember, it's important to keep your puppy occupied so that she is less likely to eat dangerous objects!

Anything within your puppy's reach is a potential hazard. Some solutions are fairly easy— for example, if you get into the habit of leaving bathroom doors closed, you can drastically reduce the number of toilet-paper-eating incidents. My Husky is particularly fond of checking if any bathroom doors are slightly ajar, and if they are, chewing her way through every item in the garbage. The bathroom can be home to plenty of other objects you don't want your dog getting into like cleaning products (my dog loves to eat whole bars of soap!), hair products, and razors. Save yourself this headache, and keep bathrooms off-limits.

You probably already know that certain human foods, like grapes and chocolate, are off-limits to your pet. As a good rule of thumb, look up any food before you feed it to your pet. The real trick, though, is to make sure your puppy isn't getting food out of your garbage when you aren't paying attention. Garbage cans that lock are a great investment to prevent messes and to keep pups from eating things that they shouldn't. This is especially important for chicken bones, which can be extra tempting for dogs but pose a choking hazard.

As with food, keep any medications, insecticides, fertilizers, detergents, and anything else puppies could potentially want to get into out of reach or locked away. Antifreeze is deadly. Batteries are also small potential hazards.

Children's toys with small parts should not be used in the same space the dog frequents. Dogs can potentially eat or choke on small parts.

If you keep plants in your house, be sure to consult your vet or check online to see whether they are dangerous. Lilies, daffodils, and tulips can all be poisonous.

Besides items around the house your dog might be tempted to eat, there are other dangers as well. Make sure electrical cords and glass objects are not within reach.

Before bringing home your puppy, there are a few items you should make sure to have to prevent last-minute trips to the pet store.

All of these rules to remember might sound scary, but once you have your house set up to accommodate your puppy, maintaining it won't be as hard! Like obedience training, potty training, and everything else with your new pup, you'll have to put in a lot of work at first to establish routines and get in the groove of being a dog parent. Soon, closing bathroom doors and locking garbage cans will be second nature, and you and your dog will both be happier for it.

Photo Courtesy of Jamie Woodhead

# Temperature and Environmental Considerations

Huskies thrive in cold temperatures, although they can adapt to warmer weather as well. Their heavy double coat protects them from the cold, and can also reflect heat.

Before you bring your Husky home, you'll want to have some kind of plan for making sure she has a comfortable area where she won't become overheated. If you live in a cool area already, great! If your area is warm year-round, or for part of the year, consider what measures you might take to keep your Husky comfortable.

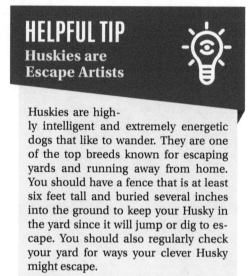

**HELPFUL TIP**
**Huskies are Escape Artists**

Huskies are highly intelligent and extremely energetic dogs that like to wander. They are one of the top breeds known for escaping yards and running away from home. You should have a fence that is at least six feet tall and buried several inches into the ground to keep your Husky in the yard since it will jump or dig to escape. You should also regularly check your yard for ways your clever Husky might escape.

During the hottest parts of the year, plan to walk or run with your Husky in the morning or evening, during the coolest parts of the day. As it warms up in the afternoon, make sure your dog has a cool place to retreat to. Air conditioning is great, although sometimes an expensive option. Huskies have been known to (at least in my experience) monopolize the vents where cool air comes out, sleeping on top of them to cool off. Having ice cubes on hand is also good, either to throw in water or to double as a toy. My Husky especially likes to bat the ice around and chase it around the kitchen floor before finally eating it on a hot day.

If it's an oppressively hot day, your Husky should really only go outside to use the bathroom. Otherwise, she should remain near the AC. If you don't have AC, or even if you do, your dog might still prefer a cooler room like the basement. Crates can also be useful here—as den animals, Huskies usually learn to like their crates and feel protected in them. Crates can also remain cooler than surrounding spaces, with a cold metal bottom that my dog enjoys. Depending on your dog, she might also love to play in the water. Many Huskies have fun at dog beaches, or running through sprinklers and kiddie pools on hot summer days. Mine does not like to go into water, but she loves trying to bite water sprayed from the hose and playing in it.

If you're really worried about keeping your Husky cool, there are some new options you could try. You can buy a crate fan, which attaches

*Photo Courtesy of Beth Gandolfo*

to your dog's crate, or just point a fan at it. A cooling mat could also help out as a nice place to rest. You could also try a cooling vest, which usually works by being dipped in water, then cooling your Husky until it dries off.

The most important thing you can do when the weather is hot is monitor your Husky and be proactive about keeping her hydrated and cool. No matter what, do not ever shave your Husky! Her coat actually helps her stay cool, and she will probably have problems with regrowth. Instead, be sure to groom your puppy regularly.

## Preparing Outside Spaces

While Huskies like to be indoors and around their family, some of them may enjoy the option of spending time outside. Definitely don't plan for your Husky to roam around freely, and don't count on an invisible fence either. These aren't recommended for Huskies, who may be determined to get out and run right through one. Instead, prepare your yard with either a fence or a leash that your dog can be attached to. If you decide to leave your Husky outdoors at all, be sure to check in frequently. Huskies are clever escape artists, so if they see a potential way out, or some small animal they want to chase, they might bolt.

Whatever your outdoor configuration, there should be some shade or covering that your Husky has access to whenever she wants. This is especially important on hot or sunny days. She should also have clean, cool water on hand.

Outdoor space is nice to have, but don't be too discouraged if you don't have a huge yard. The most important thing will be keeping your Husky active through exercise, maybe several walks a day. As long as she gets that, a yard isn't totally necessary.

## CHAPTER 4
# Bringing Home Your Siberian Husky

*"Separation anxiety can be strong in some puppies when they first leave their litter and mother. Be patient, kind, and reassuring to the new puppy. Within a couple of weeks they should settle into your lifestyle."*

**Sheri Wright**
*Bralin Siberian Huskies*

It's finally here—today you bring home your new puppy! The last chapter should have been helpful for planning ahead and preparing your family for this new member, so here we'll dive into what to expect out of those early days.

*Photo Courtesy of Andrea Martinez*

# The Importance of Having a Plan

You probably already know that bringing home a new puppy shouldn't be a spur-of-the moment decision. Instead, you'll want a plan in place before you pick her up.

Before you get her, you should have an idea of how you'll want to start introducing your Husky to your family, home, and life. Who will come to pick her up? Who will be home when she gets there? Who will be around the first few days or week?

This is also a good time to figure out what spaces your puppy will and won't be allowed in. Decide where her crate will go, and where her bed and toys will be. You might decide to block off part of your house with her things for a while, so she can get comfortable and acquainted with just this small area at first. It might also be easier to babyproof just this small section at first, and make it totally safe, with nothing she can get into trouble with. Choose a room near the center of your house, where people will be, so your pup doesn't feel lonely or left out. Jill Campbell, a breeder at Campbell's Siberian Huskies, says Huskies "Really want to always be with a human," so be sure to facilitate plenty of contact, even if the pup is limited to certain sections of your home.

If a certain room is off-limits, or the pup won't be allowed on furniture, everyone in your house should be on the same page. If you start implementing these rules the moment your puppy comes home, you'll have a much easier time making them stick.

You can also develop plans for a routine that your puppy can learn to expect and rely on. Figure out who will feed the puppy and when, who will be responsible for taking her outside, and who will handle scheduling appointments and keeping track of vaccines. Setting the expectations in advance will help ease the transition for everyone.

Finally, as a caveat, having a plan is important, but that doesn't mean you can't be flexible and spontaneous too! Keep your plan about how you want to introduce your puppy to your life in mind, but don't be too stuck on exactly how things will go. You never know how the puppy might react, and you should feel confident adjusting your plan to your specific situation. Remember, you can't control everything, so the most important thing is making sure that your puppy is healthy and safe. Everything else can come from there.

# The Ride Home

This is it—you're taking your Husky home! Riding in the car is probably new for your puppy (like most things), so you'll want to take some steps to make the trip as easy and stress-free as possible for her.

More than one person should be along for the trip so that they can sit with and comfort your dog during the ride. Your puppy might be nervous during the new experience, and you want to avoid that nervousness becoming a full-blown phobia. You or another member of the family should sit with the dog to soothe her and speak in a low, comforting voice. Hold her and prevent her from jumping on the driver.

Depending on your car and what will fit, you could put your puppy in her crate for the ride home to get her used to it. If you do this, make sure to secure the crate so it's not sliding around the car!

*Photo Courtesy of Hollye Rack*

# The First Night Home

When you first bring home your puppy, the key thing to remember is calm. A car ride, new people, and an unfamiliar environment are all likely to stress out the pup. You can help her adjust by speaking in a quiet voice and handling her gently. Avoid yelling and rough play.

Potty training begins now. Before you bring her inside, take your dog to the area outside that she will be using. If she goes, praise her. Be prepared to take her out regularly after this, including throughout the night. Continue to take her to this same spot to establish it as her potty place.

The first night should be the beginning of establishing your routine, so don't invite any friends over to meet the puppy just yet.

Bring your puppy into the room with her crate, which you'll

*Photo Courtesy of Bobbi Sharon*

want to introduce immediately. This area that you've blocked off for her will serve as her "den" for the first few days she's home with you. After that, you can gradually allow her to explore more of the house, with supervision. For now, keep her on a leash inside.

Sit on the floor or couch (if you plan to allow her on furniture) and gently pet her and talk to her. You want her to get to know your voice and how it feels to be petted, and eventually feel comfortable with that. If everything is going well and the puppy isn't too stressed out, start to touch her paws, examine her ears, and rub her belly. The earlier she can get accustomed to these touches, the better, so that you can eventually play with and pet her, or examine her for problems. You can even try grooming her gently with a soft brush to get her used to that sensation as well.

Put bedding and some chew toys or treats in the crate, maybe also a shirt or towel with the scent of her mother and littermates. Providing

Photo Courtesy of
John Sieber

something familiar will help your puppy feel comfortable while everything is new. Let her spend some time in the crate so she can process and rest from all the stimuli you've thrown at her.

After 15 or 20 minutes of playing, the puppy should go outside again to potty. Take her out last thing before bed, and first thing in the morning, and plan to get up during the night as well.

Remember to check with the breeder to find what brand of food your dog is used to eating, so that you can provide the same. If you do intend to switch to a different food, possibly on the advice of your vet, transition between the two over a period of a few days. Huskies tend to have sensitive stomachs, so you'll want to avoid introducing too many new things at once.

When you're ready to go to bed, place a treat and the shirt or towel with the mom's scent inside the crate. Don't respond to whining or barking; that will only reinforce the behavior. Tell her good night, and then go to bed yourself. If the crate is in your bedroom, the sounds of your breathing and sleep movements can calm her.

Remember that puppies don't yet have good bladder control, so expect some accidents. Think of the puppy as a new baby—she will require patience and kindness, because everything is new to her.

# First Vet Visit/Choosing a Vet

Jill Campbell of Campbell's Siberian Huskies recommend that owners

"Have a vet chosen and first appointment made before even taking puppy home." This appointment should be within 48 hours of bringing your puppy home, to confirm that she's in good health. Depending on your contract with the breeder, they may even require that you take your puppy within a certain time period of bringing her home.

If you don't already have a vet you like, ask your breeder for a recommendation. You can also find options through breed groups in your area, or by asking a friend. Ideally, you will find a vet who you are comfortable talking to, and who you can see for the entirety of your dog's life.

The first visit will likely just be a physical and weigh-in. This will allow your vet to establish a baseline of what is normal for your pup, and also allow her to be handled by other people and develop some positive associations with visiting the vet. You may schedule more vaccinations.

# Pet Supplies to Have Ready

Having a dog can be expensive, especially at first. You'll want to be ready with most of the basics, knowing that you might have to add things or change them up once you have your puppy home and see what works. At least try to have everything on hand that you'll need during the first few days, and then you can always buy more from there.

**HELPFUL TIP**
**Pet Insurance**

While Siberian Huskies are a relatively healthy breed with few genetic conditions, they are highly prone to eating things they shouldn't and escaping from yards to be hit by cars. Pet insurance plans don't cover preexisting conditions, and many have waiting periods after you sign up before the coverage goes into effect. As a result, you should sign up for pet insurance as soon as you bring your Husky home, so it can go into effect before you need it.

Let's start with the basics: you'll need ID tags for your puppy with her name, your name and phone number, and your vet's name and phone number. Attach this to a sturdy collar and six-foot leather or nylon leash (ideally one that can't be chewed through).

Okay, collar and leash are taken care of. Now you need food and dishes to go with that. You'll want stainless-steel food and water bowls,

Photo Courtesy of Christina Moore

so that they won't absorb odor. Picking out a food may be a bit tricky. Wendy Bentley, a breeder at Sweetgum Siberians, says, "Some Siberians do tend to have sensitive stomachs a little more than some other breeds. In this case, you should talk to your veterinarian about what kind of foods they think would be good for your dog." To avoid this, you should be prepared with the food that the breeder was feeding.

You'll need a large crate where your dog can rest and be comfortable when you're not around. You might also want a dog bed for her to hang out on around the family.

Everything will be really new and interesting at first, but remember that Huskies need to stay mentally active or they'll get bored and destructive. Breeder Bonnie Schaeffel of Liberty Siberians recommends, "Get very heavy duty toys, such as Kong toys. They are likely to destroy most stuffies. Give them bones to chew." Be prepared with a variety of toys to see what your pup prefers. These toys will be especially helpful when your pup starts teething. Bones and Kongs are definitely good choices; my own dog can spend hours working on a toy like that, but she's been known to destroy a stuffed animal within minutes, pulling out stuffing and eating it.

As far as grooming, you'll want to make sure you have a brush for your Husky's coat. You don't have to start grooming her right away, but it's good to get her used to the sensation early on. Dog shampoo, toothbrush, and toothpaste will round out your grooming supplies, and don't forget nail clippers.

Finally, make sure you have treats ready! Feel free to break them up into tinier portions— you'll want them around to reward the pup when she does something right, like going potty outside.

# Cost Breakdown for the First Year

Here is a very general breakdown of costs you'll face in the first year of owning your Husky. These numbers can vary greatly depending on where you live, whether you got your dog from a breeder or shelter, and any medical issues that arise.

| | |
|---|---|
| Siberian Husky | $1500 |
| Spaying/Neutering | $70 |
| Initial Vet Exam | $70 |
| Collar/Leash | $35 |
| Crate | $70 |
| Training Classes | $145 |
| Food | $120 |
| Toys and Treats | $50 |
| License | $15 |
| Pet Health Insurance | $225 |
| Miscellaneous | $50 |
| **Total** | **$2350** |

Remember, this is just a rough estimate to keep in mind around how much you might plan to spend on your first year as a Siberian Husky owner. Expect all of these costs to vary based on your location and preferences. As a good rule in general, expect some other unexpected costs to come up. Prone to destruction as they are, don't be surprised if you have to replace a couch destroyed by an overactive Husky.

# CHAPTER 5
# Being a Puppy Parent

In this chapter, we'll give you some tips and strategies to help adjust your new pup to your home and prepare for a successful relationship. Any dog will take some time to adjust to new circumstances and rules, so hopefully this guide will make the transition as smooth as possible.

## Standing by Your Expectations

Photo Courtesy of Hannah Henson

As we've mentioned before, the first few days with your new puppy are some of the most important—they show your puppy what he can expect to get away with, what he can expect to be rewarded for, and how the routine will go.

Everyone in the household, along with any visitors, must be on the same page about your expectations. If you don't want a dog that spends his life begging for food, or trying to snatch it off the table, you can't allow it from day one. Even when confronted with the sweetest puppy-dog eyes in the world on day one, you must resist. That goes for little kids too! If even one person is susceptible to begging and whining, the dog will realize and come back to them, again and again. This goes for just about every rule you want to establish. Pups not allowed on furniture? Don't allow it, even on the first day.

# How to Crate Train

*"Don't let the excessive crying prevent you from properly crate train-ing your puppy. Siberian Huskies can be overly dramatic."*

**Sheri Wright**
*Bralin Siberian Huskies*

You probably already know the benefits of crate training. As we've discussed in earlier chapters about bringing your puppy home, the crate can be a place of rest for your pup. It can serves as a bed, and since it's enclosed, the crate can also be a safe retreat from pestering children or too much excitement. Alternatively, a crate can also be a safe place to put an overactive pup so he doesn't get into anything dangerous when you aren't around to supervise him.

Photo Courtesy of Paige Whiting

Finally, the crate will be a great tool for you in potty train-ing, which we'll address in the next chapter. If your pup sees the crate as his bed, that's help-ful because dogs are very reluc-tant to go to the bathroom in their bed.

The first step to effectively crate train is choosing the right crate. Ideally, it should be large enough for your dog to walk in, turn around, and lie down, though not so big that he can potty on one side and sleep on the other side. Of course, your Husky is going to grow, so you'll want a crate that will accommo-date his adult size. Some large crates come with partitions so that you can block off the ap-propriate amount of space as your puppy grows. Jill Camp-bell of Campbell's Siberian Hus-kies recommends a coated wire

crate as a place for the puppy to be alone, because Huskies get too hot in plastic crates.

Before you lock your pup in his crate, it needs to be familiar and hopefully not too scary. It's best to already have the crate set up when you bring your puppy home, so it's simply part of the furniture in the room. Leave the door open, and allow him to sniff and explore.

Next, work on making the crate welcoming and appealing. Line the crate with a good blanket or dog bed. You can also throw a toy your pup likes playing with into the crate, and allow him to chase after it. Consider placing a blanket over the top as well, to mimic a den environment.

Going in and out of the crate freely is a good start. Then you want to train your pup to tolerate staying in the crate with the door closed. One method that tends to work well is using treats. Show your pup one of his favorite treats. Let him smell it and taste it. Once you've really got his attention, throw it in the crate and close the door, with the puppy on the outside. When he's crying and begging to get into the crate, let him in and close the door behind him. Leave him in there for a short period, around ten minutes, then let him out and immediately take him out to potty. This way, you'll ingrain the idea that good things can be found in the crate, and it will be associated with positive experiences. You can also establish a routine of potty time immediately after the crate.

# Begging

Just about all dogs beg. It's their natural reaction to food—if it's there, they want it. With training, you can discourage this behavior and prevent the pup from annoying or harassing your family and guests at mealtimes.

The most important thing you can do to discourage begging is not to give into it. Rewarding begging, even infrequently, can undo your training and reinforce the behavior. Huskies in particular are smart, and they will figure out if there is one member of the family especially likely to fall for the begging routine. Wendy Bentley of Sweetgum Siberians recommends, "Never feed them human food. Once they get the taste of human food, they may become extremely picky." I've experienced this with my own Husky. We became a little too liberal with the treats, and soon she was turning her nose up at plain dog food, waiting for us to add human food on top. This was a wakeup call, and we all decided to be more strict with our "no rewarding begging" rule.

Be vigilant at home in not rewarding begging, but don't let up when you're away from home, either. Remind all visitors and friends that you don't give your begging pup treats. This can be really hard, and you might even feel mean, like you're denying your pet. Remember, you feed him two meals a day! He isn't starving, and in fact you're looking out for his health. Many dogs in the United States are overweight, and by feeding your Husky a healthy diet you're helping him avoid health problems.

*Photo Courtesy of Kelly Rycroft*

Photo Courtesy of Carolyn Kline

Beyond just not rewarding begging, you should not pay any attention to your dog while he attempts to beg for a treat. Don't look at him, talk to him, or do anything else that seems like it might eventually lead to a treat. This includes reprimanding him—that's still attention! It's better to just let the behavior pass, and reward him with treats at other times.

If your dog is around at mealtimes, he probably begs and tries to sneak up onto the table. To curb this behavior, start a new routine where he waits in a different room while you eat. This won't be easy, and probably won't take right away. You might need to use a baby gate, at least at first, to keep him out of the kitchen or dining room. After you finish eating, go to your pup and reward him with snuggles and treat. You want to establish the message that staying quietly in his place while you eat will yield the best results for him. You might also consider leaving him with a treat like a Kong filled with something he likes while you eat, to distract him.

Finally, and this applies to just about every behavior you want to curb or encourage, be patient. Your puppy is still learning how to live with you and testing boundaries. He won't change overnight. Don't be surprised if it takes a while to see any difference, even if you are as consistent as can be.

# Chewing

Puppies love to chew on just about anything, and Huskies are no exception. Especially at first, when everything is new and you've just brought him home, keep an eye on your dog. Do not give him the run of your house unsupervised, or you're setting yourself up for destroyed belongings. Liane Tofani from Midnight White Siberians says, "If you don't want it chewed, don't leave it laying around." Until you have established some boundaries and feel confident your pup knows what he is allowed to chew, don't give him the chance to destroy anything valuable.

Your dog might be chewing for any number of reasons. He's testing boundaries, bored, or maybe he just wants attention.

To start enforcing good chewing behaviors, you should provide your dogs with some toys that he is allowed to chew. Make sure that they're distinguishable from non-chew household items—don't give him an old sock or T-shirt and expect him to know which socks are his and which are yours!

While your Husky is learning the rules, always supervise him. It's a good idea to keep him confined to a small area, like one room that is puppy proofed with water and chew toys. The crate can also be a good place to temporarily get away from chewing temptations.

Keeping your pup mentally and physically stimulated is key to stopping chewing. Jess Moore of Jalerran Huskies says, "They need some sort of daily exercise—a walk at least. But, don't forget that mental stimulation can be as important as physical exercise, as these guys are very intelligent." The more time you can offer a Husky playing with people, the better. The same goes for walks, puzzle toys, and anything else that will use up his energy. Remember, any energy that doesn't get burned off in playtime will be used on your home and belongings! Of course, exercise should be based on age, so don't overdo it with a young puppy, but Huskies will behave best when they're tired out.

If you have a pup who has a particularly bad interest in chewing, you might want to look into taste-deterrent products like bitter apple. You can spray them on items your dog is prone to chewing (like a leash). Be sure to observe them, though. Some dogs don't mind the scent, or even like it. My Siberian, for example, loved nothing more than chewing on her leash. We coated it completely in bitter apple spray, which didn't bother her at all, but made our entire household gag every time we breathed it in.

As far as what not to do, never chase your dog to take whatever he is chewing. To him, being chased by you is a fun game! You don't want to reward chewing behaviors with playtime and attention. Instead, call your pup, or offer a treat in exchange.

Don't punish your dog if you find something he chewed up hours or even minutes ago. Unless you catch him in the act, it won't do much good and he won't understand why you're mad at him. If you do manage to catch him, firmly say, "Drop it." When he drops the off-limit item, you can offer a treat or other chew toy. Praise him when he chooses the toy over something that he shouldn't chew on.

# Howling and Barking

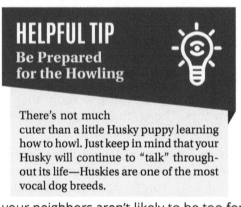

**HELPFUL TIP**
**Be Prepared for the Howling**

There's not much cuter than a little Husky puppy learning how to howl. Just keep in mind that your Husky will continue to "talk" throughout its life—Huskies are one of the most vocal dog breeds.

If you're an experienced Husky owner, you probably know about their propensity for howling. Siberian Huskies rarely bark compared to other breeds, possibly because barking is often territorial and Huskies are very non-territorial. If your Husky does bark, it's likely at something like an animal. You probably won't have to worry much about barking, but your neighbors aren't likely to be too fond of howling.

No one really knows why Huskies howl, but we know a few things that can inspire them. Howling is a way to communicate, but what is your pup trying to tell you? He might be bored, hurt, want attention, or simply be in the company of other Siberians. In other words, howling can signal just about anything, which isn't all that helpful for you. Here are some strategies to interpret why your pup is howling.

If howling is accompanied by whimpering, or seems to occur even when you're not around, that's a sign that something could be wrong. Check out your dog, and take him to the vet if necessary.

It's far more likely that your dog is howling for attention. As social animals, Huskies don't like to be left alone for extended periods. You might hear howling when they are left in their crate, or any time that they have to be separated from the rest of the family for some reason.

Much like begging, howling and whining are often cries for attention, and rewarding them only encourages the behavior. While you should never attempt to totally silence your dog (dogs make noise! Don't get one if you can't make peace with that!), there are ways to discourage the behavior through training. When your pup starts howling, whining, or whatever his preferred sound is, just let him go. Don't attempt to silence him, just let him tire himself out. When he finally stops (be warned, this may take a while), immediately say, "Quiet," or whatever word you plan to use, and give him a treat. If you can diligently do this, he should eventually start to associate "quiet" with not howling and then getting a treat. Again, this doesn't guarantee your dog will never howl, it's just a tool to keep it from getting out of hand.

# Digging

Huskies love to dig. In the wild, dogs will dig to find water, follow the scent of animals or insects, build dens, find shade, or just because they are bored. As a pet in your yard, your dog probably doesn't have any of these needs, but the drive is still there. Husky paws are perfect digging tools, and if you don't watch out you can have a mess or an escape on your hands.

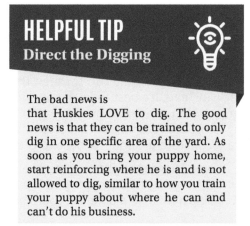

**HELPFUL TIP**
**Direct the Digging**

The bad news is that Huskies LOVE to dig. The good news is that they can be trained to only dig in one specific area of the yard. As soon as you bring your puppy home, start reinforcing where he is and is not allowed to dig, similar to how you train your puppy about where he can and can't do his business.

To stop your Husky from digging, consider what might be motivating him. Is he hot? If he's outside and it's even moderately warm, you should provide some shady spots for him to lie in and escape the sun. You could also give him a kiddie pool or some source of cool water to play and rest in.

If your Husky is a persistent digger, he might be bored or have extra pent-up energy. Like chewing and other behaviors you want to discourage, exercise and play will tire your dog out and make him less destructive.

Your Husky might also just really like digging! Some dogs will dig no matter how much exercise you give them, or how many other toys they have. If you want to give your pup a safe outlet to dig, you can make a sandbox or pit in your yard and allow him to play there.

# Running Away and Escape Attempts

Maybe you've seen some famous Husky escapes online, where dogs leave home and end up hundreds of miles away, reuniting with their families against the odds. Huskies seem to show up in these stories a lot—they really love to escape!

Siberians are natural-born escape artists, but you can take some steps to prevent escapes. We already know Huskies are pack animals, and don't like to be left alone for long periods of time. If they are, they'll try to escape and find some company, so make sure that they have some interaction during the day.

They could also try escaping if their energy isn't being used up, or they are bored. To remedy this, make sure your dog has a variety of toys to keep him busy. He should also get daily walks and play with his family every day to keep from having too much extra energy. Staying in the backyard alone doesn't count as exercise; Huskies still need walks and other forms of play!

Huskies have a strong prey drive, so if they see another animal that they want to chase you'll be hard pressed to deter them. This is what makes invisible fences such a bad idea for Huskies—they're too strong-willed, so they'll likely run through the fence and be reluctant to come back. Instead, it's best to keep your dog inside when you're not home or around to supervise. If he is going to be left outside without you watching him, a six-foot fence is generally the recommended height. You'll also want concrete around the base to prevent digging.

Some Huskies might be experts at slipping out the door when you're coming or going, so be aware of this as well! You might establish a routine of closing him off in a different room before anyone opens the front door.

# Bedtime

Trying to sleep through the night with a new puppy can feel like sleeping with a newborn baby. It's a good idea to exercise a few hours before bed, so that your pup will be tired, but not still wired from playing.

Right before bed, make sure he has peed and pooped. This will maximize the amount of time before he wakes you up to go again. Don't forget to reward him when he goes!

Crating your puppy is a good way to solidify a bedtime routine, and will also help you in potty training. Put your pup to bed when you go to bed, and place the crate next to you. Hearing you breathe will comfort your pup and help him feel less lonely for his mom and littermates.

The crate should be comfortable, with some kind of blanket or dog bed for him to snuggle with. It's also a good idea to provide chew toys, which can be a comforting way for the puppy to wind down before sleeping.

As we discussed before, your puppy will not want to soil his bed, so if he has to go he will likely fuss. Pay attention to your pup's specific way of telling you he needs to go, whether it's whining, stomping around, or something else. Until you know his way of showing you, be cautious and take him out at any sign of fuss. Remember to reward him for letting you know he needs to go!

When you do get up with him, remain calm and gentle. You don't want to give the impression that it's playtime. Expect to wake up a few times per night with him, and probably wake up early as well.

## Leaving Your Dog Home Alone and Separation Anxiety

A puppy should never be left home alone all day, but at some point you will need to leave him home alone for shorter periods of time. Your goal here is to avoid creating separation anxiety, and make your comings and goings as insignificant as possible.

As soon as you bring your puppy home, you will begin to establish routines that he will take notice of. He will probably start to recognize your morning routine, and may get anxious at any sign that means you're leaving soon, like your alarm clock. To counteract this, you want to slightly disrupt your routine every day. Don't pick up your keys last thing each morning, and try to vary eating breakfast and getting dressed. The less time he has to get worked up because he realizes you're leaving soon, the better.

When you leave, it's also a good idea to distract your puppy so he's not totally focused on you. A few minutes before you leave as you crate him, give him a Kong filled with peanut butter, or some other favorite treat. He will hopefully focus on that and miss that moment when you leave.

The most important part of not creating separation anxiety is committing to low-key entrances and exits. It's tempting to pet and kiss your pup as you leave to remind him you love him, but that just sets him up to be sad and anxious when you do leave. Similarly, when you come home you probably want to shower him with attention immediately. These are both bad ideas! You don't want to establish your comings and goings with major events and sources of affection for him. Counterintuitively, it's actually best to ignore him for a few minutes when you get home. Then, feel free to play with him and show him attention.

## CHAPTER 6
# House-Training

*"Potty training can take up to 6 months for some, but typically takes around 3 to 4 months. It all depends on how consistent you are."*

**Wendy Bentley**
*Sweetgum Siberians*

## Different Options for Potty Training

Potty training might be the part new puppy owners fear most, with good reason. Even in a best-case scenario, expect to wake up during the night, get up early, and clean up plenty of messes. But don't worry! It's completely doable.

# The First Few Weeks

Potty training begins as soon as you bring your puppy home. You don't want to establish bad habits that will take time to break, but you can instill good habits in your pup from day one.

Photo Courtesy of Kirstin Henry

We've mentioned confining your Husky a few times already. Again, this is crucial. Instead of giving him the full run of your house, baby gates can make it easy to block off just the family room, for example, so your pup can spend time with his pack without getting into trouble. While he's confined to just this room, you can keep a close eye on him, not giving him the chance to potty where he's not supposed to. Unsupervised time means time that he can make mistakes and go in the wrong spot, setting back your training.

You should preempt his need to go potty, taking him out first thing when he wakes up, and immediately after eating and drinking, as well as every so often even if he hasn't done any of those things. Eventually, you'll be able to recognize signs that he has to go, but at first he'll have nearly no bladder control. Breeder Wendy Bentley of Sweetsum Siberians says, "Watch for signals from your dog before they go to the bathroom. They will let you know in different ways they must be taken out. Each puppy is different."

Consistency is the best thing you can do for your pup regarding potty training. Always take him out the same door. Bentley suggests, "Be very consistent where you take them. Choose one area in your yard to take them to and tell them to potty." As you do, say, "Outside?" or some variation of that which you'll be able to keep using. At first, he might get distracted on the way out, so be prepared to carry him to his potty spot. Note that you shouldn't do this every time, or he won't develop the routine of needing to go, walking outside, and using his spot. When you're outside, let him wander around for a few minutes; he may go again!

If you've been consistent with taking him out, your pup should begin to expect to be taken out after eating, waking up, or playing. "Dogs work best when they have a routine," according to breeder Bonnie Schaeffel of Liberty Siberians. This is a great step on your way to a fully house-trained dog.

To prevent nighttime accidents and minimize taking your dog out, limit water about an hour before bedtime. This also means you shouldn't allow any vigorous play right before bed, since he won't be able to get a drink.

# Rewarding Positive Behavior

**HELPFUL TIP**
**Crate Training**
**for Success**

Using a crate to help house-train your Siberian Husky is an excellent way to set your dog up for a lifetime of success. You never know when he may encounter a crate or kennel in the future–at the vet, groomer, or doggy daycare, for instance–and you want your Husky to be as comfortable as possible with the experience.

When you're trying to make potty training stick, praising your pup is key. Pet him and speak lovingly to him when he potties where he's supposed to. Treats are also a good reward. You especially want to reward him when he starts to let you know he needs to go out by "dancing," whining, or going to the door.

The other side of this issue is punishment. Ideally, there will never be anything to punish, because you'll keep such a close eye on your pup and anticipate his need to go every time. Realistically, there will be some accidents, but they aren't the end of the world. As Jess Moore of Jalerran Huskies puts it, "If the puppy has an 'accident', it's not their fault ... it's yours." Be aware of where your puppy is developmentally—for some time after you bring him home, he just won't be capable of controlling his need to go, or telling you what he needs. Instead, it's on you to keep an eye on him and give him plenty of chances.

Like with chewing, it can be really frustrating when your pup makes a mess or destroys something you care about. Don't yell at him or seem angry, though. If you catch him in the act, you can correct him. If you react angrily, he'll only learn to go inside the house when he's outside of your sight. If you find it later, any punishments won't register as related for him. Take it as a sign to pay closer attention next time.

When accidents do happen, cleaning them up thoroughly and immediately is crucial. You definitely don't want your pup getting the idea that it's okay to have waste lying around. If you don't clean the spot well, it may still smell of urine, and your pup could think that's the new spot to go.

*Photo Courtesy of Crystal Mills*

# Crate Training for House-Training Use

*Photo Courtesy of Izai Sanchez*

Like we mentioned in Chapter 5, your crate is the best tool you have for potty training. If you can make the crate appealing and comfortable, your pup will enjoy his time in there and regard it as his space. Dogs naturally don't want to soil their space. Anytime you can't supervise your pup, he should be in the crate.

When he's in the crate, your pup shouldn't have room to use one corner as toilet and still lie down. This will sabotage your potty-training plans. Instead, he should have room to turn around and lie down. When he has to go in the crate, he might be distressed because he doesn't want to go potty in his bed. Any whining, pawing the floor, gnawing on the crate, or other upset behavior can indicate that he has to go. If you can take him when he does that, and reward him for going outside, you're on your way to establishing good potty habits. As your pup gets better at this and accidents become less frequent, this behavior will transfer over to the larger space he is confined to, and eventually to indoors in general.

## FUN FACT
### AKC Ranking

According to the American Kennel Club (AKC), Siberian Huskies are the 12th most popular dog breed in the United States.

CHAPTER 7
# Socializing with People and Animals

Now that we've covered the basics of getting your puppy comfortable in your home and with your family, it's time to think about socialization more broadly.

## Importance of Good Socialization

Puppy socialization is another important step that you definitely don't want to skip. This period has the most effect on how your dog will react to new people and pets for the rest of her life, so you want to get her out in the world and exposed to new situations between seven weeks and six months. In this window, exposing your pup to new sights, sounds, and smells will allow her to be less fearful of these things as she grows. Missing out on this critical period of growth might mean your pup is never really comfortable in the world, leading to anxiety, fear, or aggression.

Photo Courtesy of
Amy Junes

The whole idea behind socialization is to prevent fear and problems later in life. Although some dogs are just naturally timid, this period can largely determine whether your pup is afraid of riding in the car, or wary of children. A socialized dog has better coping skills, so she's better able to adapt to new or scary situations as an adult, and less likely to react with aggression.

It should be easy to understand why you'll prefer a well-socialized dog. If you ever plan to have company to your house, you don't want your dog to be a deterrent because she can't handle people in his home. You definitely don't want to worry on every walk that she might get spooked by another dog or person on your path. If you're adopting a puppy today and plan to have kids in the future, even minimal interactions with babies and children as a puppy will make your life much easier in the future.

Photo Courtesy of Joelle Brown

Socialization can also have a direct effect on the health of your pup. Poorly socialized dogs make a vet appointment much more difficult. If a dog is struggling, it's much harder for a vet to evaluate its heart and lungs, and muzzling a dog during an appointment makes it nearly impossible to examine dental health.

# Behavior Around Other Dogs

*"The most important tip for any breed of dog, including a Siberian is to know that dogs will go through four emotions when encountering another animal. They will Fight, Flight, Avoid or give Submission. The ONLY one anyone should ever correct is Fighting. Do not baby them if they are being a bit shy, let them deal with it on their own."*

**Liane Tofani**
*Midnight White Siberians*

Opportunities to socialize your Husky with other dogs will probably come up naturally on walks, but it can't hurt to make sure these encounters happen through trips to the dog park or enrolling in a puppy training class. You can also bring your dog to a local pet store, where you're likely to run into some other dogs in a controlled environment.

When you do encounter other dogs, it's important to have treats ready. Any time your dog has a good interaction with another dog (and good can be a sliding scale, depending on your dog's progress), make sure to reward her with her favorite treat.

In every interaction, follow signs from your dog. Greetings between pups should be long enough for them to get acquainted, but not so long that your Husky gets worn out. A tired dog is more likely to be aggressive or act out of character. As you get to know your pup better, you'll get better at recognizing when she's starting to get tired or needs a break. It's a good idea to err on the side of caution, so if you're not sure, it's okay to step away.

Use your common sense. While you eventually want your dog to handle all interactions with other dogs with ease, start out easy. Another puppy, or a dog that you know is friendly, is a safer bet than the unknown. Don't introduce a giant Great Dane to your tiny puppy right off the bat, either. She might be easily intimidated. Always make sure the other dog is friendly before facilitating a meeting. Signs of discomfort, like excessive panting or yawning, are also a sign to cut the interaction short.

# Properly Greeting New People

You can start getting your pup used to meeting new people right away. It's important not to overwhelm her by starting at a busy public place, but having friends stop by is an easy way to get some new people into your pup's life. Frequent short meetings with new people are better than prolonged meetings, so she has a chance to rest after being overstimulated.

## HELPFUL TIP
### Curbing Jumping

Huskies are so enthusiastically friendly that they tend to jump on everybody they meet. Teaching your Siberian Husky to sit nicely when it meets people is crucial since people can be frightened or angered by having such a large dog jump on them. Never reward your Husky with attention for jumping on you—turn your back and ignore it, instead.

While your Husky is still young, inviting a friend or two at a time over to meet her is a good idea. There won't be as many distractions or other new things to check out, since she's on her home turf. Huskies aren't usually very territorial, so you shouldn't have to worry about that. Be sure to give your puppy treats to make sure she associates friendly meetings with good things!

Photo Courtesy of
Jennifer Charlton-Dennis

# Huskies and Children

Like with all introductions we've covered so far, supervision is important. This goes double for children—you want to be on hand both to make sure that they don't accidentally hurt the puppy, and that the puppy doesn't become aggressive. Be extra vigilant for signs of agitation in your pup, or that she needs a break. Kids, especially younger ones, can make quick and unpredictable movements that are stressful on a dog. If they've never met a child before, they might not know what to make of it at first. Before playing with children, your Husky should already have exercised and used up some of her energy.

Before and during the introduction, help your children understand how they should treat the puppy. Remind them not to jump or move towards the puppy too quickly, because it might scare her. Be prepared to separate them if the kids decide it's funny to pull on the pup's tail or ears. Don't let them tease the dog either.

Talk to kids about biting, and warn them that the puppy might nip them. Tell them what you say when she bites something she's not supposed to, and show them how to redirect her attention to a toy. Depending on their age, you might let them give her a treat for good behavior. You can also remind them that Huskies love to play, so they might jump or bat at them, but it doesn't mean they're being mean. Puppies are still learning their strength and how to play with people.

No matter how well they interact together, never leave a baby or small child unattended with your Husky. Even the sweetest dog can accidentally hurt a baby simply with her size and strength.

Huskies are very affectionate, and they can make wonderful family dogs and be very patient with children. Obviously, this depends on the temperament of your dog, but with careful introduction and teaching kids to understand how to act with her, the introduction should go well.

# CHAPTER 8
# Huskies and Your Other Pets

Integrating your Husky into your house and family includes introducing her to your other pets and making sure that they're comfortable together. Most of the tips we've already suggested so far will apply here as well, so being consistent and supervising playtime is still important.

## Introducing Your New Puppy to Other Animals

If you have other dogs already, you'll definitely need to manage your expectations. Sometimes people think that their older dogs will welcome the pup with open arms and act as a mom or dad. Unfortunately, this isn't very realistic, but there are steps you can take to make the introduction as smooth as possible.

Puppies don't always know all the same rules that adult dogs do. They are accustomed to playing with their littermates, who probably wel-

*Photo Courtesy of
John Sieber*

64

come being rudely awakened or played with at all hours. An adult dog probably won't react so kindly to this, which your puppy will pick up on and learn from.

As we've mentioned, the dogs should meet in neutral territory, somewhere that isn't your home. That way you lower the risk of the older dog acting territorial and intimidating your pup.

There are alternative ways to introduce the dogs, and you could also do several of these to ease their relationship

## HELPFUL TIP
### Introducing Your Husky to Other Pets

Since Huskies are bred to be pack animals, they tend to be friendly with just about any animal they meet (unless they were poorly socialized as puppies). With that being said, your other pets may be less enthusiastic about the new family member jumping all over them. Take your Husky for a long, tiring walk before introducing him to your other pets to help reduce his energy levels and encourage a calm meeting.

along. The leash could make your dog nervous, especially the puppy, if she feels like she can't get away from the big scary dog. Instead, allow the dogs to meet unleashed through a fence. Then they can sniff each other freely without really meeting nose to nose. This is especially a good idea if there's a significant size difference between the pup and the older dog. Then some of the excitement can wear off before a high-energy meeting.

Another option is parallel walking for the first meeting. Take both dogs for a walk, each handled by a different person, and walk them parallel to each other. Don't let them stop and stare at each other face to face. Don't hold the leashes too tightly, and give them some slack to move around, but keep the dogs far enough apart to be out of sniffing distance at first. Use treats or toys to keep them interested in you, rather than the other dog. Walk them for five or 10 minutes, and assuming there's no tension, let them greet each other and sniff. Every few minutes, call the dogs separately for treats or toys to prevent tension from building and to create positive associations. Limit this first meeting to about 10 minutes, so that the dogs don't become overtired.

Early in the relationship, you should be on the lookout for signs of discomfort or aggression. Alternatively, there are signs that things are going well too! If the dogs want to play together, that's great. Body language like a bow, when the dog's tail end goes up and front end goes down, is a classic invitation to play. Even if there is some barking and growling, this can be a normal part of play, as long as you keep an eye on body language. Allow play for only a few minutes to make sure no one gets too tired.

Photo Courtesy of Ruby Jenkins

If you have multiple dogs, the puppy should meet each of them one on one. Once this has happened and the meeting was positive, they can all meet again in your home. Ideally, your other dogs should be otherwise occupied while you bring the puppy inside. Then the other dogs should enter to find the puppy already there. It will likely take time for them to

## FUN FACT
**Blue Eyes and More**

Huskies are known not only for their beautiful blue eyes, but they're one of the breeds most likely to have two different-colored eyes. They can also have eyes that are each both blue and brown!

all figure out where they stand in regards to each other and how to interact, so keep the puppy separated from the rest when you aren't around to supervise.

Now that we've talked a bit about socializing your pup with other dogs in earlier chapters, you might want to introduce her to your other pets. In particular, you might be thinking about how she will adapt to living with pet cats.

When the new puppy meets your cats, you'll want to control the environment closely. They should meet in a neutral location to prevent aggressive or territorial behavior from either. You'll already be working on confining your puppy to small areas of your house while she learns the rules. Let each pet have turns alternatively confined to their space and roaming more freely, so that they can explore the new scents. When no one is home, pets should definitely be confined separately until they've had more time to establish a relationship.

Once both animals seem calm and eat normally, you can make leashed introductions. Let them greet each other, keeping your Husky on her leash. If either dog seems aggressive or overly irritated, cut the meeting off. Continue like this until both animals seem relaxed and don't really take much notice of each other. When you aren't home, they should still be separated.

Finally, after about a month of positive interactions, you can allow them together unsupervised.

# Pack Mentality

Siberians retain many of their ancestors' instincts, including a strong pack mentality. In a human-dog pack, you'll want everyone to understand their place.

In a wolf pack, there are traditionally three positions in the hierarchy: alpha, beta, and omega. Dogs begin learning their places in this order from birth as they establish their place in the litter. Usually there is one alpha male and female that lead the pack. Then there are a few betas that are subservient to them. The rest of the pack are omegas, subservient to everyone. When you have one dog, you are the alpha. It's especially important with an independent and smart breed like Huskies that they recognize all of their human family members as above them in the hierarchy, or you could find yourself with all sorts of behavioral problems. Huskies will be happier and less stressed if you lead with consistency and confidence. If you're willing to bend the rules, or the rules aren't really clear, your pup might be stressed and attempt to take control. When she knows you're in charge of dinner time, when she can play, and other things, then she can relax.

If you have more than one dog, then there are really two packs—one with you and the dogs, and one of the dogs. In the dog pack, one dog will

*Photo Courtesy of Michael Brosko*

be dominant and the others will be submissive. It shouldn't be too difficult to spot these roles. The dominant dog might push her way to be first through doorways, take the best sleeping spot, or seem jealous when you show attention to the other dogs. Submissive dogs will likely follow the other dogs, give up toys and sleeping spots, and not maintain eye contact. Your job with this pack hierarchy is not to interfere with the positions (as long as no one is getting hurt!). You can do this relatively easily by feeding the dominant dog first, putting her leash on first, and generally doing things in pack order. If you upset the order, the dominant dog may feel insecure about her place and begin to exhibit aggression.

# Fighting and Bad Behavior

Dogs that otherwise get along fine might sometimes veer from playing into what looks like fighting, and this can be fine. However, it's not okay to let your dogs carry on serious aggression. If fights seem like long ongoing disputes, rather than isolated incidents caused by specific things each time, you might have an aggression problem. Fighting that draws blood, or seems intended to cause harm, is a problem. Fighting should stop when one dog submits to the other. If your dogs are fighting in small isolated incidents, you can correct them, separate them, and use some of the earlier introductions to reset things between them. Whether you can successfully correct dogs with deeper aggression towards each other depends on how long the behavior has been going on, the intensity of the aggression, and how many fights they've had.

The longer any of these have been going on, the less chance you have of permanently fixing things. With strict supervision, you might be able to prevent fighting, but you likely won't end the tension between them. If you learn to recognize situations that are stressors, you can minimize or deescalate before they become full-blown fights.

Fights can also occur when dogs are challenging each other for social status. This is especially common when a new dog is added to the pack. Supervision and respecting established positions can help deter this behavior.

Finally, try to keep some consistency and routines that your dogs can rely on. If your home feels chaotic and the dogs lack supervision, their behavior and interactions can deteriorate.

# Raising Multiple Puppies from the Same Litter

While it's possible to successfully raise two puppies from the same litter (I've done it!), it's generally not recommended. The common wisdom about dogs from the same litter is that they may develop "littermate syndrome," meaning that they are so deeply bonded with each other that they won't bond as strongly with their human family, and they may develop an unhealthy emotional dependence on each other.

*Photo Courtesy of
Babette Dickinson*

Being away from each other, even briefly, can cause extreme emotional distress, and their excessive time together means that they may lack social skills to interact with other dogs. This has the side effect of making them harder to train as well. They are often so caught up in playing with each other that they can't be bothered to learn simple obedience commands.

The other reason potential owners are usually warned about adopting puppies from the same litter is aggression. They might have very strict roles in which one is dominant to the other, and prevents the other from playing or getting attention.

If you do decide to adopt littermates, it's important to keep them separated much of the time, especially as puppies. This is when they develop the ability to be alone, so separating from their sibling isn't a traumatic experience. You'll also need to commit to training them separately, playing with them separately, and taking them on individual walks. Basically, getting two puppies at the same time will add extra work and time, but if you do it carefully, it can be done.

## Options if Your Pets Don't Get Along

Once you've exhausted all of these tips for introducing pets, sometimes there isn't much you can do if two dogs' natures are just at odds with each other. Increasing their exercise is a good idea as an outlet for some energy that won't be used fighting. If this doesn't help, you should consult a dog trainer or specialist to come and give you expert help.

You should also work with each dog separately on training, especially deference and commands to "leave it" about whatever she is doing (including fighting).

If even bringing in a professional doesn't work, then for the safety of your family and your pets, you should separate them. This doesn't have to mean just giving up one of them, however. If you know of someone who might be a good home for your dog, meet with them to see how they interact. If you can't ensure a good home for your dog, you should give her to a shelter, or contact your breeder to see if they are willing to take the pup back. Your vet may also know of a breed-specific rescue, or someone looking for that type of dog.

# CHAPTER 9
# **Physical and Mental Exercise**

*"Siberian Huskies need at least an hour or two of good exercise every day. Some good exercise ideas include walking with your dog, jogging, biking with your dog, carting, hiking, swimming or playing with other dogs."*

**Wendy Bentley**
*Sweetgum Siberians*

You might be sick of hearing it by now, but we'll say it again: Huskies need plenty of exercise! This is as much for your well-being as it is for theirs. If they don't get the physical and mental exertion that they need, you'll definitely feel it. A Siberian without mental stimulation or physical exercise to tire him out is likely to entertain himself by digging through your yard, eating your valuables, and howling.

*Photo Courtesy of Izai Sanchez*

# Exercise Requirements

Like we've talked about, Siberians are working dogs, originally bred for pulling. They are strong, lean, and agile. They are high-energy dogs, so they require at least an hour of exercise per day, ideally more when circumstances allow.

A daily walk is essential for your Husky. Walks are great for your pup because he can work off some of his energy while also stimulating his mind with new sights, sounds, and smells.

Your Husky would probably be happy to walk all day, so he's only really limited by your time and stamina. A walk of 30 to 45 minutes is a good baseline to aim for, or you could go for two shorter walks. Your individual dog's needs will vary, but generally a tired Husky is a good Husky.

When you're figuring out an exercise schedule, it's important to re-member that your pup will do best with a routine. A 30-minute walk at the same time every day will work out better than nothing all week, fol-lowed by a long, strenuous walk on the weekend.

# Dealing with Pulling

*Photo Courtesy of Canvas Foxwell*

Huskies are bred to pull, so you'll definitely want to work on training your dog out of this behavior. Harnesses are great because they make it tougher for your pup to pull, but training is still necessary.

The easiest way to train your dog out of his pulling habit is by rewarding him for paying attention to you and walking next to you. You want to give your dog the idea that walking next to you is a good experience, and reinforce this idea with treats and pets. At the beginning, use really special treats that your dog doesn't get often.

If your goal is to get your dog to follow your lead in walks, try holding his leash and taking a few steps backwards. He will probably follow you, so say "yes" or "good boy," or whatever positive reinforcement you use as he does. Immediately reward him with a treat.

Another way to work on this is by holding a treat in your fist and letting your dog follow the treat and walk along with you. When he does, give him the treat. After he has successfully done this a few times, have him follow your empty fist. Again, reward him with treats.

74

# Different Types of Exercise to Try

Just about anything that gets your dog moving and using up energy counts as exercise, so you have plenty of options beside walking. Of course, along with walking, feel free to try jogging or running if you're up for it, depending on your dog's age. A full-grown Husky will appreciate the chance to up his speed.

If walking is a little too boring or monotonous, try hiking. You'll get exercise benefits, plus your dog will love the opportunity to explore new sights and smells, and potentially other animals.

Swimming can also be a good exercise outlet for dogs, especially because it's easier on the joints for older pups. Not every dog likes to swim, so this depends on your dog's personality. If he likes going in the water, great! Encourage playing in the water with toys or treats. If your dog isn't enthusiastic about getting into the water, that's okay.

*Photo Courtesy of Jana Polivka*

Playing fetch or frisbee can also be a great way to get your dog exercising. This can work in your yard, or at an enclosed dog park. For extra exercise, walk your dog to a separate location and let him explore, then engage him in a game of frisbee, being sure to throw far away. The park is especially great because playing with other dogs is a sure way to use up some extra energy.

If your dog has a lot of extra energy to burn off and walks and playtime aren't cutting it, consider joining an agility group. A quick Google search should help you find one in your area, and there you can direct your pup's physical and mental energy to learning tricks. If you live in the right conditions, you could also try training your Husky to pull a sled.

# Safety

Although they love exercise, it is possible to overexercise your Husky, especially a puppy or senior dog. They can keep going beyond what they can handle, especially in hot weather.

Puppies' bones and joints are still growing, so you should avoid strenuous exercise. Any activity that is tough on your pup's joints could cause lasting damage. Instead, he should be allowed to play freely with toys and other (friendly) dogs. As he grows, short walks are okay, although they should be more for getting your pup used to being on a leash and sniffing around the neighborhood. An easy rule to remember is about five minutes of exercise per month of age, so a three-month-old puppy only needs around a 15-minute walk.

When you do walk your dog of any age, keep an eye out for signs of an over-tired dog. If he shows excessive panting, extreme thirst, is acting out of character like lagging behind, or is limping and reluctant to continue, you should end your walk early and keep an eye on him. Be sure to provide water, too.

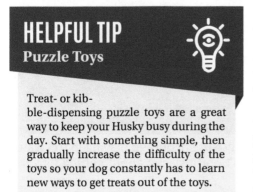

**HELPFUL TIP**
**Puzzle Toys**

Treat- or kibble-dispensing puzzle toys are a great way to keep your Husky busy during the day. Start with something simple, then gradually increase the difficulty of the toys so your dog constantly has to learn new ways to get treats out of the toys.

With Huskies, it's important to keep an eye out for overheating, especially in the warmer months. Limit exercise to the early morning and evening, when temperatures might be a bit more moderate. Offer water frequently, and listen to your dog—if he doesn't want to go, it's too hot for him. Watch out for increased heart rate, excessive heating or drooling, and being warm to the touch. These are all signs of an overheated dog.

# Importance of Mental Exercise

We've said that a tired dog is a good dog, but physical exercise isn't enough. Any dog, but especially a smart Husky, is likely to get into mischief if he is bored or not getting to use his brain as much as he'd like. Of course, like all of the advice here, this depends on your dog. You know him best. If he's consistently destroying things in your house or acting out, consider mental exercise as a possible solution. It doesn't have to be particularly complicated, just enough to make him work a little.

# Tips for Keeping Your Husky Occupied

*"Siberian huskies exercise well in their own fenced yards, especially if they have a companion they can play with. If you don't have such an environment you should walk your dog at least twice a day in the morning before you go to work and in the evening when you return. Be careful about too much exercise when it's very hot outside and make sure there is plenty of freshwater available."*

**Sheri Wright**
*Bralin Siberian Huskies*

There are so many ways to add mental stimulation for your pup, and anything related to food is a great way to start. Mix up his eating routine, and make him work for his food rather than just setting it down in front of him. There are plenty of toys out there that require interaction with your dog to dispense food, like in a ball or Kong that he has to play with to get food out slowly. Your dog will be motivated by the food and will use up physical and mental energy working for it.

You can also let your dog explore and lead when you're on walks. Let him stop and sniff when you're walking. Going on a walk is a major excitement in your dog's day, and he gets a lot of stimulation from being able to take in the scents of the environment and other animals. Dogs will usually be more tired after a walk that includes opportunities to sniff and wander around.

Puzzle toys are also good ways to entertain your dog, even for a few minutes. That's enough to make a difference. The type of toy will depend on your dog. For example, my Husky loves a Kong filled with peanut butter and will spend hours trying to get every little bit out.

You can also teach your dog new tricks to expend some mental energy. You'll increase impulse control and focus. For example, teach him the names of his toys, and get him to the point where he can bring you a specific toy. Tricks like this, that he has to work hard for, will tire him out.

## CHAPTER 10
# Training Your Husky

*"10-18 weeks is Boot Camp Time! That's when we recommend to start obedience training.  As like any other breed of dog, this is the imprinting stage and all the effort and training you put into the puppy during this time is what they will hold onto as an adult. TOUGH LOVE is important and Freedom is earned NEVER given."*

**Liane Tofani**
*Midnight White Siberians*

Training your Husky begins on day one, and you want to set expectations from the first moment. Training doesn't have to be difficult or take over your life. Here are some basics that should help you establish the rules with your pup.

*Photo Courtesy of Nikki London*

# Operant Conditioning Basics

Operant conditioning is the idea of training your dog through rewards and punishment for certain behaviors. It's probably what you intuitively think of when you imagine training a dog.

Photo Courtesy of Mirta Calixto

This idea comes from psychologist B.F. Skinner. The main takeaway from his theory of operant conditioning is the idea of reinforcement, meaning that if a reward encourages a behavior and a punishment discourages behavior, repeating these effects solidifies the association. Dogs respond to this association. For example, your dog will likely soon learn that when you pick up his leash, it means a walk is coming soon. The leash itself won't make your dog happy, but he is able to associate it with the walk to come, and therefore he becomes excited upon seeing the leash.

The important thing to remember about operant conditioning is awareness about what behaviors you might accidentally be rewarding. This will become especially important for begging, whining, barking, and other behaviors you want to nip in the bud.

# Primary Reinforcements – Food, Toys, Playtime

Your best tools to reinforce good behaviors are things that your dog already likes. Primary reinforcers are things that your dog is born needing or wanting, like food or toys. These will always be a clear way to communicate to your dog that you like what he was doing. Food is the clear winner, but you don't want to always use it. Be sure to save your dog's favorite foods, and food rewards in general. If you keep them special, they will pack more of a punch.

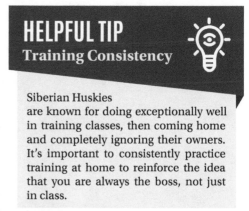

**HELPFUL TIP**
**Training Consistency**

Siberian Huskies are known for doing exceptionally well in training classes, then coming home and completely ignoring their owners. It's important to consistently practice training at home to reinforce the idea that you are always the boss, not just in class.

Photo Courtesy of
Angie Mullins

Toys and playtime will also reinforce good behavior. For example, waiting until your pup is calm and not begging, before you take him for a walk, is a good idea. Then he won't learn that he gets rewarded for begging and going crazy before a walk.

# Secondary Reinforcements – Attention, Praise, Clickers

Secondary reinforcements are things that your dog can learn to associate with primary reinforcements; think praise or clickers. Of course, you'll have to work to form this association, so that your dog learns "good boy" is a good thing for him! You'll begin by using secondary reinforcers in conjunction with primary reinforcers, so every time you praise him,

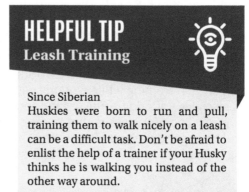

**HELPFUL TIP**

**Leash Training**

Since Siberian Huskies were born to run and pull, training them to walk nicely on a leash can be a difficult task. Don't be afraid to enlist the help of a trainer if your Husky thinks he is walking you instead of the other way around.

he also gets a treat. To really solidify this association, condition the secondary reinforcement as if that is a behavior that you want to encourage. Eventually you can use the secondary reinforcement without the primary, but do so sparingly. If you want reliable behavior, don't totally eliminate the primary reinforcement association. You can phase it out over time, but every so often be sure to accompany your praise with a treat.

# Dangers of Negative Reinforcement

Negative reinforcement, or training your dog by punishing him for doing something you'd rather he didn't, might seem tempting or necessary for a well-behaved dog. Unfortunately, training isn't always as easy or intuitive as it seems. You might have the impulse to punish your dog with, say, time in the crate, after he pees in the house. However, unless you catch him in the act, he won't associate the punishment with the action you want him to avoid. If anything, you'll only teach him to hide and pee in the house when you're not around. Punishment like this will also create negative associations with his crate, which you want to avoid. The crate should be his space where he feels comfortable, so it can't double as a punishment.

# Hiring a Trainer/Attending Classes

Training your pup can be tough and time-consuming, so it's tempting to outsource the job to someone else.

Some owners might consider hiring a trainer to take care of training their pup for them. This might work for some owners, but you should consider the potential risks and rewards. You definitely need to be involved in the training process yourself if you want your dog to understand that you are in charge and that he should listen to you. If you decide to hire a trainer, be sure that they envision a situation where you are an active participant in the training. They should also have years of experience, and have a background working with Siberian Huskies.

Attending classes is another option, and they're a great way to get guidance in training while working with your dog. As a nice bonus, classes also give your dog some great opportunities for socialization with other pups. Look for classes that meet once a week for about eight weeks, and have good reviews. The teacher of the class should have been working in the field for a while, and have successful examples to point to.

Photo Courtesy of
Hannah Johnstone

# Owner Behavior

Finally, it's easy to forget your own role in training as the owner. Your behavior matters too! Your pup will be focused on you, your demeanor, and your reactions, so try to be aware of these, especially in training scenarios. If you're stressed or upset, your pup will definitely pick up on it, and training will become stressful for him, too.

Another important thing to remember in your own behavior as you train your dog is not to ascribe human behaviors to him. Remember, he did not make a mess or disobey you to make you angry. He doesn't think like a human. Reminding yourself of this should help you deal with exasperating situations more appropriately.

*Photo Courtesy of
Cassie Burgos*

# CHAPTER 11
# **Basic Commands**

*"Huskies are easy to train, as they are very smart. However, it's their smarts that also give them their stubbornness. Just when you think you have them fully trained, they may test their boundaries. It's important to stick to your guns and make sure they know that you are in charge, not them."*

### **Andrew and Heather Kronenberger**
*Frosty Meadow Husky Farm*

Some basic commands, along with potty training, will make up the bulk of your training. A short overview of each should give you some guidance to get started.

Photo Courtesy of
Jess Gowan

# Benefits of Proper Training

There are many benefits to training your pup properly, some more obvious than others. Puppy classes are a great way to give your dog opportunities for socialization that aren't overwhelming, and will also use up plenty of Husky energy. The mental stimulation, both from interacting with other dogs and from learning commands, is also good for your dog. Siberians are smart, and they want to be challenged, so challenge them!

**HELPFUL TIP**
**The Importance of "Drop It"**

Siberian Huskies can be very mischievous. Watching a video of an owner chasing their dog around because it stole their keys is hilarious—being that owner chasing your dog with your keys when you're late is not so funny! Make sure you train your dog to have a solid "drop it" to maintain your sanity—and your dog's health in case it picks up something dangerous.

A better-trained dog gives you better control of her, which is helpful in many ways. You'll be able to take your pup out in public more easily, without worrying about how she might act, and you'll be able to have guests in your home without having to always accommodate her. Training her gives her the tools to interact with other people and animals, and she will feel safer as a result. This is obviously good for your own social life, but your pup will benefit as well! Dogs are social animals, and Huskies especially love to be around their families. The more you can integrate her into your life, the happier you both will be.

Training your dog properly can even save her life, in the right set of circumstances. Even the best-behaved dog could run away if she gets scared, but if she will come back to you when called, you could save her from running out into a busy street or during an evacuation for a natural disaster, for example.

Working with your dog on training will also help you develop a stronger bond. Through the process of training, you'll build trust and respect between each other. As a result, she will also likely be more confident and relaxed, because she knows how you expect her to act in a variety of situations.

Photo Courtesy of
Lindsay Rhodes

# Picking the Right Rewards/Treats

Choosing the right treats will make your training much smoother. First of all, think about the size of a treat. You want something that your pup can eat quickly and resume training. This is likely much smaller than a typical commercial dog treat, something about pea-sized is ideal. Then your dog can quickly enjoy the treat without getting distracted from the task at hand and spending time playing with her treat. Buy tiny treats, or feel free to break up larger ones into small pieces.

Small treats are important to keeping your dog healthy, too. If you're training regularly, your pup might be eating many treats in one day, so you don't want to inadvertently make her overweight in your attempts to praise her! She shouldn't be consuming enough treats to make her full. Remember, treats aren't replacements for meals.

Soft, smelly treats are a great choice for training rewards. They are faster to eat, and won't leave your dog crunching and looking for crumbs on the floor. As a bonus, most dogs prefer stinkier, smellier treats. If you want to really solidify a positive association with a behavior, go for this kind of treat. It's also a good idea to change up your treats, keeping your dog guessing and preventing her from getting bored. Then she never knows what reward will get her a favorite treat.

# Different Training Methods

There are so many methods for training your dog, and you'll find different recommendations from breeders, veterinarians, and trainers who've had success with each. Here, we'll give a brief overview of a few different methods, which will hopefully help you make your decision.

One potential avenue to follow is the alpha dog, or dominance, method. For this method, you should embrace the idea of your family as a pack, and your job is to ensure that your dog sees you as the alpha. This generally requires that you not allow her on furniture with you or get down to his eye level. Some experts aren't fans of this method—it's often described as outdated, with the understanding that dogs aren't as reliant on pack mentality as we previously thought. This method can also be stressful for both you and your dog, because it requires constant maintenance of your status as alpha.

Purely positive reinforcement is another method which we have largely been following so far. To follow this method, you reward good behavior, and don't acknowledge bad behavior. The only punishment is removing rewards, like toys or treats. This method also requires consistency, and everyone in your household will have to be on the same page.

You might also be interested in trying clicker training, which is similar to or even an offshoot of positive reinforcement. The idea here is that you use a clicker to indicate to a dog when she has completed a desirable behavior. The clicker is advantageous over other rewards because you can pinpoint the exact moment your dog does the behavior you want to praise. Of course, the key to this method is getting your dog to respond to the clicker.

*Photo Courtesy of Rachel Hamilton*

# Basic Commands

Even if you don't plan on having the most obedient, well-trained dog in the world, a few basic commands are useful and important for your pup to know, and all dogs can learn them. Remember to keep training sessions brief, around 10 or 15 minutes.

## Sit

This is one of the easiest tricks your pup can learn, and a good place to start. There are a few methods to teach "sit," although it's important to note that you shouldn't physically put your pup into a sitting position, which can be confusing for her. Instead, stand in front of your dog holding a treat you know she enjoys. Wait for her to sit, and when she does, say "yes" and give her a treat. You can repeat this a few times, eventually starting to say "sit" while she does it.

## Stay

"Stay" is another command your dog should be able to master without too much trouble. The key to this command is duration—you want the dog to stay put as long as you say.

Choose what word you'll use to release her from the command; I like "okay," but some people use "free," and anything is fine as long as you use it consistently. Stay with your puppy while she's either sitting or standing, and throw a treat. Say your release word as she steps forward to get the treat. Continue to repeat this (using small treats!), and try saying the release word before you throw the treat and she starts moving. She should start to get the message that the release word means she can move.

At this point your dog should know "sit," so have her sit on command. Give her a treat for staying in sit, then use the release word. Repeat this, waiting longer between treats. Don't get frustrated if your dog gets up before the release word; she just wasn't quite ready yet. Gradually add more time and distance between yourself and her, and try turning your back too.

## Lie Down

You can teach "down" similarly to "sit." Like before, wait for your dog to lie down on her own. Then reward her with a treat and say "down." Then you can release her and wait for her to lie back down again. When she does, repeat what you did before and say "down" again.

You can also try using a treat to lure your dog down by bringing it to the floor. Give the treat when her elbows touch the ground. After a few times, you can try this with an empty hand. Like with "sit," never physically force your pup into position.

## Come

Teaching your dog to come when called is one of the most important skills you can teach her, and can avoid danger and worry. Start practicing this skill indoors at a time when it's relatively quiet. Sit with your pup, and say her name or "come," or both. As you say it, give her a treat. You're not asking her to do anything yet, but you want to start building associations between hearing those words and good things for her.

Next, you can drop a treat on the floor in front of your pup. After she finishes eating the treat, say her name. Give her another treat when she looks up at you. Continue doing this, moving the treat further away, or going behind her so that she has to turn to look at you.

Be careful not to say her name too frequently, or it will become something easy for her to ignore.

## Off/Down

This is the command for getting your dog off furniture where she's not allowed, along with off the people she'd like to jump on. You'll probably naturally want to say "down," but since you're already using that for "lie down," you can try "off" instead. The key is to remember to use the same term consistently.

When your dog puts her paws on someone, or does whatever you plan to use this command to correct, say "off." Show her a treat. As soon as all of her paws are on the floor, give her the treat. Don't punish her or yell at her when she jumps up on things. Instead, keep using treats with "off."

## Give/Drop

This command, where your dog will learn to open her mouth and let you have whatever she's gotten hold of, is really important for her safety. You'll be thankful you taught her this the first time she has a chicken bone or something else she could choke on. It's also a good lesson for her on not being aggressive with her toys around you.

To teach this skill, have a few objects ready that you know your dog might like to chew on, and also have some desirable treats ready. With the treat in one hand, use your other hand to get her interested in chewing on the object. Once her mouth is on it, hold the treat up to her nose and say "drop it" (or whatever phrase you choose to use). Praise her, and give her the treat while you pick up the object and give it back to her. This is an exercise you can practice throughout the day as she picks up things. Don't worry if you can't always give it back to her because it's dangerous or fragile, just follow the rest of the steps.

## Advanced Commands

Of course, if you and your pup find that you enjoy learning new tricks together, there's no reason to stop there! You can teach her to heel, roll over, speak (although your Husky is probably already pretty vocal!), and more.

## CHAPTER 12
# Dealing With Unwanted Behaviors

*"While outside, whether on a leash, on a chain, or in a fenced area, a Husky has one goal in life: To get away. It's not that they want to get away from their owner and never return, but rather they simply want to run and play on THEIR terms. They attempt to climb over, chew on, jump over, dig under, and outsmart whatever is containing them."*

**Andrew and Heather Kronenberger**
*Frosty Meadow Husky Farm*

## What is Bad Behavior in Dogs?

**FUN FACT**
**Huskies are Fast**

Huskies can run
up to 28 miles per hour!

When you bring a dog into your house, you expect him to eventually learn how to act a certain way. There are plenty of behaviors that he can learn, or which he will come into your house already knowing, that you'll want to curb. Barking, howling, aggression, digging, whatever it is, you'll likely follow the steps here to address the problem.

## Finding the Root of the Problem

Many bad behaviors in dogs stem from anxiety or aggression. They account for most undesirable behaviors, and are often contributing factors to dogs going to shelters. Pay attention to when your dog acts out—for example, does he exhibit compulsive behaviors like biting his feet? Does he start certain behaviors as you're about to leave the house? Before you can really correct these behaviors in a way that will stick, you should understand if they stem from aggression, anxiety, or something else.

Photo Courtesy of Sarah Jane Smith

# How to Properly Correct Your Dog

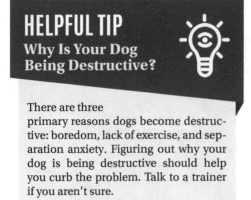

**HELPFUL TIP**

**Why Is Your Dog Being Destructive?**

There are three primary reasons dogs become destructive: boredom, lack of exercise, and separation anxiety. Figuring out why your dog is being destructive should help you curb the problem. Talk to a trainer if you aren't sure.

You'll want to think before you correct your dog, because a lot of your instincts will not be very helpful. Think about what your dog is trying to accomplish with bad behavior. Often, attention is at least a partial motivator, so you don't want to inadvertently encourage jumping up on people by reprimanding your dog whenever he does it. All he'll understand is that it gets your attention.

Give your dog the opportunity to succeed and do something good. There should be an alternative to the bad behavior. For example, it can be really hard to make a dog stop trying to hop on the counters to look for stray food, and you might never fully train him out of it. But you can tell the dog begging for food from the counter to go lie down, and when he does what you ask, give him a treat.

*Photo Courtesy of Lucy Cranwell*

Beyond this specific behavior example, you should always focus on giving your dog a positive way to respond. Some other commands you can train him in and reward him for are more likely to yield results than reprimanding him.

# Fixing Bad Habits

Like when you correct a dog's behavior, the key to fixing bad habits is providing an alternative option for your dog to react. Then, of course, you'll have to praise the other action and show him that it's worth his effort to do that instead. If he's chewing on something he shouldn't be, provide something that you're okay with him chewing on, plus treats. If he's into digging, provide a sandbox or other approved space where he can dig, and praise him for doing so.

Some habits, like begging, are extra hard to break, because if even one person accidentally feeds him, it will give him reason to continue. If you really want to break this habit, you'll need everyone's commitment to consistency. Even then, there's no guarantee he'll stop begging fully. Try teaching him commands like "bed" and rewarding him with a treat, like we discussed in an earlier chapter.

*Photo Courtesy of Ruby Jenkins*

# When to Call a Professional

There are many behavioral issues that you can handle on your own, or with the help of guides like this one. However, it's also okay to call in an expert when your dog requires someone with more experience. You can also seek the advice of your vet or breeder about whether you need professional training help. Basically, if your dog exhibits behaviors that you can't seem to curb but you can't live with, you need help. This goes double if these behaviors make you worry about the safety of your dog, other people, or other animals.

*Photo Courtesy of Jamie Woodhead*

# Husky Bad Habits

As we've already covered, Huskies have bad habits that they tend towards. They can be overeager and jump on guests. The same advice foe almost any bad behavior applies here as well. Do not reward the behavior with attention, even negative attention. Ask your guests to ignore your pup (or to do the best they can if there's a large dog jumping up on them). Give them treats to distribute only when your Husky has calmed down and has all four feet on the floor.

Photo Courtesy of
Kelly Bottin

The other bad (yet often cute or funny) habit Huskies are known for is their howling. Again, you don't want to encourage this, or you'll end up with a howling pup every time you leave home, which your neighbors likely won't appreciate. Never reward howling or whining with more attention, or by delaying your exit. Although it feels hard to say no, giving your dog exactly what he wants practically guarantees he'll try the same thing again and again.

In general, Huskies are smart, and they'll learn if certain behaviors get attention or reactions that they want. You'll have to be extra vigilant to remain consistent and not give in to begging, whining, and other bad habits.

CHAPTER 13
# Traveling with Huskies

## Dog Carriers and Car Restraints

There are a variety of dog carriers and restraints on the market to keep your pet safe in an accident. The safest way for your dog to travel is in a crate that is anchored in place with a seat belt. Of course, you'll want to balance safety with your dog's comfort, and some dogs may be anxious or more prone to car sickness inside a crate. If you don't want to fully restrain your pup, consider a mesh back seat that will prevent him from jumping up in the front and keep him in one place without fully restricting his movement. This is what my family always uses with my Husky, and although she doesn't like that it prevents her from jumping into the front seat, it gives her enough freedom of movement to look out the window and lie down for a nap.

## Preparing Your Dog for Car Rides

*Photo Courtesy of Sheila Bowman*

Some dogs love riding in the car, and others seem to get carsick no matter what. Some dogs get nervous, while others love it. My Husky will try to jump in any car with an open door and tag along for a ride, but the dogs I owned before her were always nervous in the car. Your pup might never like riding in the car, but you can take measures to make car rides seem normal to him by introducing them early, when he's a puppy. Get your Husky used to riding in the car by letting him sit in it in the driveway. You can also provide a treat to entice him to hop in, or keep him enter-

# HELPFUL TIP
**Seatbelt Harnesses**

As tempting as it is to let your dog roam free in your back seat while you drive, he can become a projectile in an accident, potentially beheading you on his way out the windshield. Keeping your dog in a crate or seatbelt harness could save both of your lives in case of an accident.

tained. Then move on to short car rides. If all goes well, feel free to move on to longer rides, with the caveat that an extended road trip should probably come only after you're confident your dog can comfortably handle shorter rides.

Your best bet to prevent car sickness in your pup (even if he's an experienced passenger) is to have him travel on an empty stomach. You should make sure he has frequent access to water, though. You probably know your dog and his ability to wait best, so make a judgment about how often to stop for potty breaks. Keep in mind that to be safe, you should stop a bit more frequently than you need to. At potty breaks, offer water and give your dog the chance to walk or run around and stretch his legs.

Fresh air flow is also important to keeping your dog comfortable and preventing car sickness. If weather allows, crack a window to let air and smells in, but not enough that your pup can stick his head out the window, which could lead to eye injuries. If your dog is in a crate, make sure that it's well ventilated. Some dogs will go to sleep given the chance on a car ride, but it's still a good idea to bring along some favorite toys to prevent boredom on long trips.

*Photo Courtesy of Jennifer Kruse*

Photo Courtesy of Hannah Orman

# Flying and Hotel Stays

Flying with your Husky will be tough, so if you can't drive to your destination, consider leaving the pup at home. If you absolutely have to fly, there are some steps to take to make the trip easier. Most airlines allow only small dogs that will fit under the seat in the cabin. Unless your Husky is still a puppy, then this won't likely be an option. If your dog is still a puppy, traveling by plane could be extra stressful, and I don't recommend it.

Since Huskies are typically too large to fit under the seat, if you choose to fly your pup will be in cargo. Although most pets who fly in this manner are fine, it can be dangerous, and there are accidents where pets are injured or killed. Keep this possibility in mind as you make travel plans. To minimize these risks, try to take direct flights so that there is less possibility of a mix-up during transfer. Ask if you can watch your pup be loaded and unloaded from the plane, and travel on the same flight as him if possible. Also consider the weather at both your destination and the airport you're leaving from. Will it be too hot or cold? If it's summer, try to schedule early morning and evening flights for cooler temperatures.

When you fly with your Husky, be sure to carefully check all of your airline's specific requirements. Double-check that your crate meets the brand and size specifications. You should also give your pup a few weeks at home to spend time in the crate and become comfortable, reducing some stress for travel time. See your vet beforehand to obtain a certification of health, and ask them if your Husky is in good condition to fly.

Like airlines, hotels also have a variety of restrictions and rules for bringing pets. Some only allow dogs under a certain size. Before you arrive, check out the area you'll be staying in to find a pet-friendly hotel. When you find a hotel where your dog is allowed, it's important to still be respectful of other guests. Pack plenty of treats and toys, and be prepared to use the training you've instilled to minimize barking. Inspect the room before you let your pup run free, in case of wires, breakable objects, or anything else that could pose a risk. If you'll be leaving your Husky alone in the room, be sure to crate him. They can be prone to destructive behavior, especially in a new place.

# Kenneling vs. Dog Sitters

*Photo Courtesy of Kelly Bottin*

If you choose to leave your pup at home while you travel, you have a couple of options. At a kennel, you will drop your Husky off either at a dedicated dog-hotel type of place, or sometimes vet offices also have kennels. If you choose this option, you might want to ask to check out the facilities a bit first. How often do the dogs get walked? Do they get one-on-one attention? Is there outdoor space for running or playing? Are they isolated, or is there a chance to interact with other dogs? Depending on your individual dog's needs, these questions will all help you choose the appropriate kennel. Staying away from home can be stressful for pets, so if you do board, ask to send your food and treats from home, especially because Huskies are prone to sensitive stomachs and you should avoiding changing their diet during an already stressful time.

Dog sitters might come to your house a few times a day to let your dog outside and feed them, or they might actually stay at your house for the duration of your trip. This option is usually better for dogs who get nervous or anxious easily, because although you will be gone, your pup will be in familiar surroundings with all his usual toys and places to sleep. If you have an anxious dog, it can also be a good idea to hire a pet sitter who your pet has met before and is at least somewhat comfortable around. Kennels and dog sitters are both perfectly acceptable options, so you should make your decision based on what you know about your dog's personality and needs. After your first experience leaving your pet during a trip, you might be happy with the option you chose, or decide to try something else.

# Tips and Tricks for Traveling

Traveling with pets, like traveling with small children, will inevitably be more stressful because you're adding another creature that's dependent on you for food, potty breaks, and getting where you're going. Your goal shouldn't be for everything to go perfectly, just to make things as smooth as possible. In general, Huskies are really high energy, so you should plan extra exercise the day before your trip. Hopefully he will be extra tired during travel, and less likely to be anxious or restless. Also be sure to pack a lint brush, because Huskies shed plenty of hair. You can clean up your clothes, car, and even the hotel room if fur gets everywhere. Finally, take a few minutes to look

Photo Courtesy of Jackie Beeston

up vet information in the place you'll be staying and save it somewhere easily accessible, like a note on your phone. Hopefully you won't need it, but if anything seems off, you already have access to information and know who to call

# CHAPTER 14
# **Nutrition**

*"Huskies can have stomachs that are a bit more sensitive. Your food should have fewer ingredients, not more. Less is better in this case and you want the main protein to be the number one ingredient. If you are not working them hard, as in mushing, you want about 26% protein."*

**Bonnie Schaeffel**
*Liberty Siberians*

## Importance of Good Diet

In terms of diet and eating habits and preferences, Huskies are different from many other breeds. They have a comparatively high metabolism compared to other dogs their size, so they don't need as much food as you might think. This comes from their ancestry as sled dogs, where they were bred to survive on minimal nutrition in harsh temperatures.

Unlike other breeds, Huskies can be picky. Some breeds will eat as much food as you put in front of them, to the point of becoming sick. Huskies tend to be much more fickle—they won't eat if they're full, and they'll eat more or less depending on how active they've been.

*Photo Courtesy of Lindsay Rhodes*

If a Husky overeats, she's at risk of gaining weight. If she gains weight, it can be tough for her to lose weight, and overweight dogs have a shorter life expectancy. Keeping up good nutrition is important if you want your pup to have a long life where she can remain active.

You might need to put in extra effort to make sure your Husky maintains good nutrition, because they are notoriously stubborn. Huskies have distinct individual personalities, so look out for what your pup's tendencies are. They're naturally curious, so Huskies will often become bored with their usual food for seemingly no reason. It can be a tricky balance to keep your pup interested in her food without upsetting her stomach. You can try adding different types of meat, fish, or vegetables to her usual food. If that doesn't work, a small amount of cheese can get her interested in her food, but not too much, because it can cause stomach issues.

## Tendency for Allergies or Sensitive Stomachs

Huskies are known to have sensitive stomachs, which, in combination with their stubbornness and picky eating habits, can make them tough to feed. Consistency is key—once you find a food that doesn't upset their stomach, stick with it. Sudden diet changes basically guarantee a messy cleanup for you. When you need to entice your pup to eat, using the same base food with a small addition of meat, vegetables, or something else is your best bet. Incremental changes are okay, especially as you learn what works for your specific dog and what doesn't. As you try out different dog foods, this strategy is good too. Transition gradually, at first mixing in one-fourth serving of the new food with three-fourths serving of the current food, then half and half, and so on.

Some Huskies have difficulty digesting certain types of food. Many commercial dog foods have a chicken protein base. For some dogs, helping stomach issues might be as simple as switching to a lamb or fish-based food. If dietary issues persist, either not eating, or consistent vomit or diarrhea, talk to your vet. While your Husky likely has the usual sensitive stomach, your vet can help you eliminate the possibility of more serious issues and make recommendations for other foods.

# Different Types of Commercial Food

**CHECKLIST**

**Bad Food Checklist**

Here's a check-list you can print out and keep on your fridge, so everybody knows what people food should NOT be given to your dog:

- Stone-fruit pits
- Alcohol
- Dairy products
- Macadamia nuts
- Onion
- Garlic
- Coffee
- Marrow bones
- Chocolate
- Grapes and raisins
- Yeast dough
- Nuts
- Sugar
- Chives
- Xylitol (an artificial sweetener found in things like sugar-free gum or peanut butter)
- Fatty foods
- Cooked bones

Deciding on a dog food can be confusing, especially if you have a dog with a sensitive stomach. The internet is full of all kinds of advice, but it's not always helpful or backed up by evidence. The best place to get advice for your food needs is from your vet.

Commercial dog foods come in wet and dry varieties. Dogs usually love wet food, although it can be more expensive than dry food. Wet foods also often lack the variety of nutrients Huskies need, because they're mostly water. They're not the best choice for everyday meals, but they can be acceptable as a treat for special occasions.

Dry food is a more affordable option, and can also reduce tartar buildup for healthy teeth through chewing on crunchy food. Huskies need more protein and fat than some other breeds, so aim for around 32 percent protein and 18 percent fat. Look for foods with a high-quality primary ingredient of protein, like fish or lamb, which is especially forgiving for sensitive stomachs.

# Homemade Foods

Some Husky owners choose to feed their pets a homemade diet instead of commercial food. Protein should form the base of your dog's diet, but you should cook meat, which makes it more digestible. Fish, lamb, and bison are all good choices for Huskies with sensitive stomachs.

Fats and oils are also an important component of your Husky's diet. Flax seed, olive oil, and cod liver are all healthy oils which you can either cook with or drizzle over food before serving. Finally, carbohydrates should make up a part of your pup's diet as well, like fruits, vegetables, and rice. Cooking vegetables makes them easier to digest.

# People Food − Harmful and Acceptable Kinds

Dogs can eat some human food in moderation, but other foods should never be given under any circumstances. They shouldn't have chocolate, cinnamon, or onions. Macadamia nuts can also be toxic for dogs. Avoid grapes, raisins, peaches, and plums. In general, salt and sugar should be eaten in moderation. Don't give them meat on the bone, which poses a choking hazard.

Photo Courtesy of
Elena Martinez

CHAPTER 15
# Grooming Your Husky

## Coat Basics

Huskies' thick fur keeps them warm and gives them a regal and kempt appearance, but maintenance can be intimidating. They will require more work than smooth or single-coated dogs, but Husky grooming is completely manageable. Siberian Huskies have a double coat, with an undercoat and guard hair. The undercoat is usually shed twice a year, which is when shedding becomes a major issue and brushing will be most important. Lucky for you, your Husky's fur will never need to be trimmed by a groomer. Huskies are naturally self-regulating, and their fur will grow back and fall out as needed according to the climate you live in. Absolutely never shave a Husky.

# Shedding

*"Huskies blow out their coat two times per year. Take them outside during that time and brush them thoroughly. Never, ever, shave their coats. They need both coats for hot or cold days."*

**Jose Carmona**
*Carmona Kennels*

In climates warmer than their native Siberia, Huskies will shed their entire undercoat. This often happens in the spring to prepare them for the warmth of summer, and in the fall to prepare for the cold of winter. Keep an eye on the general shedding patterns of your dog, and you should notice early on when the seasonal shedding starts. The earlier you notice, the easier the process will be for both you and your pup. Increase your brushing frequency, and keep it up as needed. You can also take this opportunity to switch couch covers or other items that might be particularly at risk to extra dog fur, and maybe stock up on lint rollers.

Photo Courtesy of
Jessica Loughran

# Bathing and Brushing

If you have a Husky, you should learn to love brushing her, because you're going to be doing it a lot. The best thing you can do for your Husky's coat is to regularly and thoroughly brush her, at least once a week. Technique can make this process faster and more efficient. Begin with the undercoat, combing thoroughly away from the skin and against the direction of grown to remove any loose fur—you might be amazed at the sheer quantity of hair your pet can produce during your first shedding season. Then brush the overcoat in the other direction. The overcoat won't be shedding much, so you're just focusing on shine and detangling any knots or problem areas here. For brushing the overcoat, you might consider using an "undercoat rake" that will make it easier to remove fur and allow for new hair to grow in correctly. A good brush will keep your Husky comfortable and minimize shedding in your home. During this period, aim to brush every day if possible.

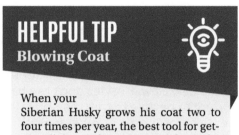

**HELPFUL TIP**
**Blowing Coat**

When your Siberian Husky grows his coat two to four times per year, the best tool for getting all that undercoat out might not be a brush. A professional-grade high-velocity dryer can blast your Husky's undercoat away without using brushes or deshedding tools that can irritate your dog's skin. Use the dryer out in your yard and send fur flying away for birds to line their nests with.

To make brushing easier in general, start introducing your dog to the feeling of being brushed early, while she's still a puppy. You can start by even just letting her sniff the brush, and rubbing it gently around her back or stomach. Ideally, brushing will become such a normal part of her routine that she won't mind, or she may even come to enjoy it.

Huskies don't need to be bathed very often, because they don't tend to produce excess oils. Frequent bathing can dry out skin and fur, so try not to bathe more than once a month. Huskies also groom themselves often, and remain relatively clean. You can go longer than a month; you only really need to bathe if your dog smells or has matted fur. When you do bathe, make sure to thoroughly rinse your pup's fur because the thick coat can hold onto conditioner and shampoo.

# Trimming Nails

The frequency with which you'll need to clip your Husky's nails depends on how much they get naturally ground down. A dog with frequent exposure to pavement will not need her nails cut as much as a dog that spends more time indoors. When you do need to trim nails, be careful of the quick. Only cut the part of the nail that looks hollow, including on the dew claw. Huskies don't like having their feet touched, but it's important to be able to trim their nails for their comfort, and also to examine them for thorns or other injuries, especially in the fur between their toes. When your dog comes in with wet or dirty feet, you can clean and dry them with a towel, which will both prevent matting and get your dog used to having you touch her feet.

# Brushing Your Dog's Teeth

With a regular toothbrush and dog-specific toothpaste, you want to give your dog's teeth a good brush about once a week. Of course, every day is ideal, but probably not realistic. Dental health is closely linked to heart health and other health factors, so it's important to stay on top of plaque as much as you can. Like brushing fur, starting this with a puppy will get her used to the process and hopefully minimize struggles. Dental chews are a good addition to regular brushing for keeping your dog's teeth clean and preventing plaque.

# Cleaning Ears and Eyes

You should make a habit of cleaning your dog's eyes with every bath, but in between baths keep a lookout for anything off. Healthy eyes should be clear, and the whites should be pure white. Some eye discharge is normal, but if you notice something unusual, including redness or swelling, contact your vet. Pawing at eyes or excessive blinking might be a sign of infection as well. Use a wet washcloth or cotton ball to gently clean your dog's ears about once a month to prevent infections. In both eyes and ears look for scratches, parasites, discharge, or anything else unusual.

*Photo Courtesy of
Andrea Martinez*

# When Professional Help is Necessary

It's okay to bring in professional help at any point. Whenever you're not sure what to do, it can't hurt to ask your vet for advice. In general, if something seems unusual and continues to get worse, whether it's an infected nail or a problem with eyes or ears, you should take it to the vet. Professional help might also be necessary if fur becomes matted or tangled.

## CHAPTER 16
# Basic Health Care

## Visiting the Vet

You'll probably see your vet most when you have a puppy and need to go in for regular checkups and vaccinations. Once your pup is about six months old (or when your vet recommends it), you can switch to annual visits. At a yearly wellness visit, your Husky will get vaccinations, and you can discuss flea and tick prevention. Your vet will also examine the dog's eyes, ears, teeth, and stools.

This is a great time to bring up any concerns you might have, even if you don't feel like they're enough to merit a trip to the vet on their own. Ask your vet about any changes in appearance or behavior you've noticed, or anything else that might have come up. Regular vet trips will also help your provider keep tabs on your dog's health, and lead to earlier recognition if something is wrong.

*Photo Courtesy of Alyssa Larson*

# Fleas and Ticks, Worms, and Parasites

Fleas and ticks are small parasites that can attach to your pup and feed off them, laying eggs and creating an infestation. They are one of the most frequent problems pet owners deal with, but it's much easier to prevent fleas than to try and get rid of them after the fact. Beyond annoyance and inconvenience, fleas and ticks can lead to more serious medical problems, and also transfer organisms like tapeworms to your dog.

Photo Courtesy of Amanda Shaffer

The variety of preventative measures on the market can be confusing, so you should definitely ask your vet for guidance at your appointment. Flea collars are not usually regarded as effective, so you will likely choose some kind of monthly topical treatment that fits your budget and needs, in consultation with your doctor. In terms of prevention, you can also minimize opportunities for exposure by keeping a well-maintained yard and limiting time spent in densely wooded areas.

# Holistic Alternatives

There are many holistic and organic treatments for fleas and ticks available over the counter, as well as preventative medications. They have been shown to often be as effective as other products. If you are interested or intend to switch to a natural product, talk to your vet to make sure that it won't compromise your dog's health.

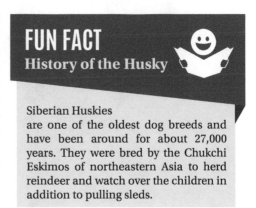

**FUN FACT**
**History of the Husky**

Siberian Huskies are one of the oldest dog breeds and have been around for about 27,000 years. They were bred by the Chukchi Eskimos of northeastern Asia to herd reindeer and watch over the children in addition to pulling sleds.

Photo Courtesy of
Dave Atchison

# Vaccinations

Vaccinations are an important part of keeping your dog healthy and are also legally required in many places. Both you and your vet should keep a record of what vaccinations your dog was given, when, and what dosage.

Vaccines for dogs are usually separated into two categories—core and non-core. Core vaccines are recommended, and sometimes legally required, for all dogs. Non-core vaccines depend on your dog's lifestyle and health, and your vet can advise you on whether they make sense for your Husky.

**HELPFUL TIP**

**An Ounce of Prevention**

When it comes to parasites, it's true what they say: "An ounce of prevention is worth a pound of the cure." Heartworm is extremely expensive and difficult to treat. Ticks can transmit diseases like Lyme Disease and Rocky Mountain Spotted Fever. Fleas are incredibly difficult to get out of your home once your dog brings them in. Keep your Husky on heartworm and flea and tick preventative treatments year-round to avoid the hassle and expense of treating your dog for parasites after the fact.

The rabies vaccines, with annual boosters, is a core vaccine. Rabies is fatal for dogs, and there is no cure. Distemper, which can cause permanent brain damage, is also a core vaccine. Parvovirus and adenovirus can also be fatal if untreated, and have core vaccinations. Other vaccines are available at your vet's discretion, for example the Lyme disease vaccine is only recommended for dogs at high risk, like those who spend most of their time in densely wooded areas. Bordetella, or kennel cough, is also a non-core vaccine, although you will likely need proof of this vaccine to board your dog in a kennel.

# Pet Insurance

Like health insurance for humans, pet insurance is a backup plan in case your pet develops a disease or injury that requires expensive treatment. In general, purebred dogs have more hereditary health conditions than mixed-breed dogs, so they are more expensive to insure. On the other hand, Huskies are not as susceptible to inherited health problems as some breeds. Insurance may be expensive for a Siberian Husky, but treatment for eye problems and hip dysplasia will also be expensive. Pet insurance also protects you in case of non-inherited health issues like broken bones or other injuries your pet might sustain.

## CHAPTER 17
# Health and Aging Dog Care

## Common Diseases and Conditions in Siberian Huskies

*"The biggest concern is with their eyes. They are notorious for eye is-sues. Having their eyes checked regularly will help detect issues. Even puppies from parents that are 'eye-certified' can develop eye issues, so it is important to obtain a health guarantee from a breeder."*

**Andrew and Heather Kronenberger**
*Frosty Meadow Husky Farm*

Unfortunately, when you adopt a dog you have to think about the future and what kind of medical conditions you might eventually face. Siberian Huskies are generally fairly healthy, but they are suscepti-ble to some of the same diseases that affect other breeds.

Huskies are at risk for a variety of eye diseases, so it's important that you check out their eyes frequently, and that your vet also takes a look at regular visits. Cataracts are one of the most common problems Huskies develop. They're like clouds that form in the eyes, and can eventually lead to blindness, affecting about 10 percent of Huskies. Progressive Retinal Atrophy (PRA) is anoth-er common problem in Hus-kies that can lead to blindness. With this condition, the retina begins to deteriorate. PRA and cataracts are both expensive to treat, but early detection can reduce costs and risks of fur-ther problems.

Corneal dystrophy is an-other eye disease that could af-fect your Husky. If your pup has

**HELPFUL TIP**
**Aging and Pain**

As dogs age, es-pecially when they are larger breeds like Siberian Huskies, the most com-mon complaint they will have is pain due to arthritis, hip dysplasia, or oth-er causes. If you notice your dog slow-ing down or limping as he ages, talk to your vet about how to minimize your Husky's pain.

Photo Courtesy of
Dan Chapp

this hereditary condition, you'll notice white dots in his cornea. Unfortunately, there is not yet a cure for this condition. Finally, uveodermatologic syndrome can affect eyes, skin, and nervous system. The skin reaction is only cosmetic and not something to worry about, but the eye condition can lead to blindness, so see your vet right away if you notice extreme redness in your dog's eyes.

Hip dysplasia is a common concern among dog owners of all breeds, and the condition is fairly common in Huskies. This condition can be both painful for dogs and expensive to treat, so it's best to catch it early, especially because both hips are often affected. Keep a lookout for some of the signs, including trouble getting up, standing with back legs unusually close together, loss of thigh muscles, and reluctance to run or jump. If you see these, talk to your vet. The condition usually appears in middle or old age, and treatment often involves surgery. Before that though, and as a preventative measure, keeping your dog at a healthy weight will make this problem less likely to develop, and reduce pain if it does develop.

Follicular dysplasia is also fairly common in Huskies, and unfortunately there is no cure. This is a condition that causes abnormal hair growth, hair loss, or patchy skin, and usually affects puppies around three or four months of age. There is no known treatment yet, but your vet can probably recommend some shampoos or topical creams to manage symptoms.

# Basics of Senior Dog Care

*Photo Courtesy of Chelsee Taylor*

One of the most important things you can do to keep your senior dog in good health is to maintain regular vet visits. You will probably notice if something drastic happens to your pet's health, but your vet will be able to detect diseases and other issues early, ideally minimizing and discomfort and cost by healing your pet quickly.

You should also monitor your dog's weight closely. Senior dogs are prone to extreme weight gain and loss, due to decreased and dental problems. Watch out for either of these, and check in with your vet to see if it's a sign of a larger problem.

Taking care of your dog's teeth is also crucial, and only becomes more important with age. Keep up regular weekly brushings, and talk to your vet if you notice any changes or problems. Dental disease can be painful and prevent your dog from getting the nutrition he needs, and he becomes more at risk the older he is.

Also keep up regular grooming. This is a good opportunity to examine your dog's entire body for changes, growths, sores, or anything else that might be concerning.

Finally, you might need some modifications in your home or lifestyle to accommodate your dog. For example, if your Husky develops arthritis, he might prefer a softer dog bed. Covering hardwood floors with rugs or carpets could also help him get his footing.

# Nutrition

Depending on your dog's health, you may need to change his food as he ages. In particular, being overweight is a major factor in many common diseases that affect senior dogs, and can make ailments that he already has more severe or painful. If you're concerned about your dog's weight, or unsure if it's in a healthy range, ask your vet at your annual visit. If your Husky does need to lose weight, make sure you're still feeding a high-quality diet that meets all of his nutritional needs. You might also fortify your dog's diet with fatty acids like DHA, which can be good for dogs with arthritis. Other specialized foods might be necessary, like a low-sodium diet for a dog with heart disease,

Photo Courtesy of
Mina Timmons

or a diet regulating electrolyte levels for dogs with kidney disease. This can be tricky to navigate, so definitely look to your vet for guidance as your dog ages.

# Exercise

Along with nutrition, exercise is your best tool to help your dog manage his weight and keep healthy joints and muscles. However, as your Husky ages you'll need to tailor exercises to his needs and abilities. For relatively low-impact indoor exercise, try some puzzle toys that dispense food slowly. These should get your dog up and moving while managing eating.

Outdoor exercise is also important, although it may look different from other points in your dog's life. Your senior dog should continue to go on a regular walks, but they should be brief. Consult your vet to see what kind of exercise levels you should aim for given your dog's age and health. If he seems to be in pain, don't try to "push through"—that's a sign from your dog that he needs a break.

Swimming can also be an excellent exercise for older dogs because it is gentler on joints. Swimming is even a recommended therapy for many injuries. As with all exercise, keep an eye on your dog and limit activities that can be fatiguing, like swimming or walking on difficult terrains.

To maintain healthy joints, you want your dog to keep moving around the house in his old age, especially going up and down stairs. If that's not an option for him, try out some ramps if he is able.

# Common Old-age Ailments

There are some old-age ailments that are common in dogs across breeds. Arthritis—the inflammation of joints—is one of these ailments and can cause stiffness and pain. It is usually managed with changes in diet and exercises and medication.

Gum disease is also a major issue for many senior dogs. Gums become inflamed when bacteria hardens into plaque. If it progresses fully to gum disease, then gums pull away from teeth and pockets are left which can become infected and lead to bone loss. This is a very serious disease, and bacteria can enter the bloodstream and cause problems for other organs as well. As a side effect, dogs may also find it difficult or almost impossible to eat, based on the progression of their gum disease.

Diabetes is another common disease in dogs, especially as they age. It can be hereditary, and is more common in females, but it can also be acquired. It most commonly occurs in dogs around eight or nine years of age. Symptoms include extreme thirst, frequent urination, and weight loss.

# When It's Time to Say Goodbye

Losing your dog is like losing a family member, and the pain and sadness can be devastating. We don't ever really feel ready to say goodbye, but at a certain point we realize it's the kindest option for our beloved pup. He might give you signs that it's time—extreme lethargy, not eating or drinking, labored breathing, etc, or maybe something unexpected happens and this decision is in front of you sooner than you expected. Either way, the most important thing is keeping your dog comfortable,

*Photo Courtesy of Timothy Sharng*

and not prolonging his suffering. Remember, he's relied on you for everything, and now he's relying on you to make saying goodbye as painless as possible.

Hopefully this is something you've talked about with your vet, but this is a good point to research what options are available in your area, and what you feel comfortable with. Do you want to take your dog back to his usual vet to be put to sleep? Is there someone who makes house calls? Will the vet keep him for cremation? Whoever you end up with should be a professional who, unfortunately, deals with this kind of situation all the time. They should understand that you're hurting, and be able to help you make the appropriate decisions.

Lightning Source UK Ltd.
Milton Keynes UK
UKHW021441020821
388088UK00001B/9